FOR THE SAKE OF ZION

FOR THE SAKE OF SAKE ZION

TUVIA BOOK

A CURRICULUM OF ISRAEL STUDIES

הסוכנות היהודית לארץ ישראל
Jewish Agency for Israel

TUVIA

"I don't know whether I've mentioned that I've become a Zionist. This word stands for a tremendous number of things. To me it means, in short, that I now consciously and strongly feel a Jew, and am proud of it…One needs something to believe in, something for which one has a whole-hearted enthusiasm. One needs to feel that one's life has meaning. That one is needed in this world. Zionism fulfills this for me."

(Chana Szenesh 1921–1944)

Contents

Contents

Contents

TUVIA

Shalom!

This updated and revised educator's guide is intended to provide students with a sense of pride and understanding of modern Zionism and its achievements.

Once Jewish students leave the protective bubble of school, home or intimate social group and enter the "real world" of a mixed college campus, sometimes hostile to Jews and Zionism, they often find themselves uncomfortable, on the defensive and unable to speak about Israel, in part because they lack the knowledge of and passion for Zion.

In order to respond effectively with a sense of self-respect and to be proactive, students need commitment and pride, as well as knowledge and tools. The units in this guide are structured to paint broad-brush strokes of Zionist literacy and focus on heroic men and women who helped shape the Zionist dream. This is a curriculum of "Identity Zionism." There are many "triggers" that should lead to passionate group discussion and debate. The clips on the suggested films listed in the index will enhance many units. It is recommended that this course be taken in conjunction with, or as a precursor to, a college activism piece such as the excellent curricula available from AJC , Jerusalem U, AIPAC and "The David Project." Most importantly a visit to Israel , preferably in a peer group educational touring program is the most effective method to develop a clear understanding regarding the achievements and challenges facing Israel.

In addition, the educator should also utilise the resources provided in the appendix in order to develop a comprehensive course on Israel that will provide the students with the specific responses to challenging questions. The appendix includes:

1. A chronology
2. A bibliography containing recommended books to enhance each unit
3. A list of suggested films to accompany each unit
4. A list of useful educational websites

The units are structured in the following manner:

*   The first pages of each unit are the educator's guide (blue stripe on top), followed by the student worksheets (grey stripe on top).
*   The first three units are foundation units dealing with the necessity to define Zionism in the twenty-first century. This involves exploring our historical and religious connections to the Land of Israel.
*   The next four units concern the rise of the modern Zionist movement and the *Yishuv* (pre-state Israel). Streams of Zionism will be reviewed as well as the *Chalutzim* (pioneers) and the hope and betrayal of the British Mandate era.
*   The culminating units relate to the Modern Jewish State, including Israel at war and peace, and acknowledge the importance of having a Jewish country of our own after almost two stateless millennia.

"For the sake of Zion I will not hold my peace,
and for the sake of Jerusalem I will not be silent..."
(Isaiah 62:1)

"...לֹא אֶחֱשֶׁה וְלִירוּשָׁלַ͏ִם אַחֲשֶׁה לֹא צִיּוֹן לְמַעַן"
(ישעיה סב:א)

Tuvia Book

"Zionism finds in it, for the Jews,

a reason to raise their heads,

and, taking their stand upon the past,

to gaze straightforwardly

into the future."

(Justice Louis Brandeis)

"The 'Z' Word"

MISCONCEPTION: "Zionism is a form of racism" (UN resolution 3379).

REALITY: "Zionism is the ancient/modern ideology which express-es the legitimate yearning of Jews the world over for their historical homeland – Zion, the Land of Israel" (Neuberger).

MISCONCEPTION: North American college campuses are havens of toler-ance and understanding, where one can express one's views without fear.

REALITY: Many North American College campuses are turning into a battleground dominated by a violent radical form of Islam that is intensely anti-Jewish and anti-Israel with the result that many Jewish students are in a state of bewildered fear.

Objectives

- Attempt to define "Zionism."
- Become aware of the current opposition to Zionism and its negative result on university campuses.
- Understand why it is necessary to define one's Zionism in order to be a self-assured Jew.

TUVIA

A: Introduction and Motivation

1. Explain that before 1948 it was easy to define Zionism – 'The wish to establish a Jewish State in the Land of Israel.' Now that the Jewish State has become a reality the question is: "What is Zionism and how does one define it today?" Does one have to live in Israel to be a Zionist, or is financial support enough?

2. Hand each pair of students Worksheet #1 (Definitions of Zionism).

3. Students will work in pairs and rank every statement from "A" (I strongly agree and/or this is very important to me) to "E" (I strongly disagree and/or this is of no importance to me).

4. After dividing statements into groups A–E ask what common factors, if any, link the statements in each group.

5. Discuss students' responses. Have them explain their choices. Ask each student to write a statement (in one or more paragraphs) about why s/he is a Zionist, using points that were raised during the discussion. A conclusion could be that to be a Zionist one has to *do* the most that one can, to the best of one's ability, for Israel.

6. Lay out the plan for the course of study.

B: Examining Current anti-Zionism / anti-Semitism on College Campuses

1. When the students have completed their statements, ask: "Why is it so important for us to deal with the issue of the definition of Zionism? How will it help us to understand who we are?" Inform the students that: "It is very possible that when you enter college a year from now, you will be entering a battlefield. A war is being fought on campuses against Israel and Zionism that often descends to crass anti-Semitism. If anyone thinks that this is an exaggeration, let us now examine the following two sources."

2. Hand each pair of students Worksheet #2 ("University of Michigan"). Ask students to read and try to respond to the questions. (Please note: it is not necessary to belabour the issue now). Inform the students that the next source is very disturbing, but it is important to confront these issues.

3. Hand each pair of students Worksheet #3: ("Violence at Concordia University"). After the students read the letter, ask them to respond to the questions. Suggestion: show the Jerusalem U film: "Crossing the Line 2, The New Face of Anti-Semitism on Campus."

4. Conclude by saying: "These are just two of the numerous campuses in North America and Europe where similar scenarios are played out. You will agree that we need knowledge, correct information and tools to advocate for Israel. The main goal of these units is to provide you with both the information and the passion for advocacy."

5. Natan Sharansky stated:"Today the battle which takes place on the campuses is one in which our enemies try to convince Jewish students that in order to be part of the world of justice and freedom, you have to disengage yourself from Israel and from your own identity. These attacks and double standards and slander result in the fact that many young Jews don't want to have anything to do with their Jewish identity. Our history, whether talking about 2,000 years ago, or the struggle of Soviet Jewry, or where it is today, you find this again and again. It's something that we have to bring to every young Jew. If you want to be part of the world of freedom and justice and *tikkun olam*, your identity is your source of strength to fight for those things – your identity, which is based on your history, on your traditions and of course on your connection to Israel." *

---

* Natan Sharansky, Interview with the Jerusalem Post, July, 2010

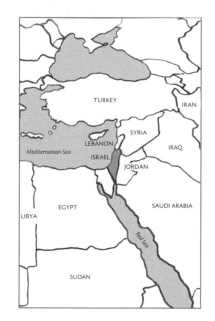

Israel in the Middle East
The Jewish State is almost exactly the size of
(1) Wales – about 21,000 sq. km. or 12,600 sq. miles
(2) The Kruger National Park in South Africa
(3) The State of New Jersey

C: Conclusion

"In the face of a vicious assault on Israel's legitimacy, it is crucial these days to understand the depth of the Jewish attachment to Israel." *

– Gil Troy

Since the Arab world is trying to negate the Jewish historical claim to Israel, it is vital for us to understand our historical and current claim to Israel. The next two units will focus on our historical and religious connections in order to answer the question, "Why Israel?" For the sake of Zion and ourselves, we need to regain pride and strength. We become empowered through knowledge. Israel needs to be an integral part of our being all the time, not just in times of crisis. The famous 18th-century Hasidic rabbi, Rebbe Nachman of Breslav, succinctly summed up this point by stating, "Every place I go, I am going to Israel."

TUVIA

"Every place I go,
I am going to Israel"

(Rebbe Nachman of Breslav)

"באשר אני הולך
אני תמיד הולך בדרך הולך ישראל"

(רבי נחמן מברסלב)

---

* Troy, Gil, *Why I am a Zionist: Israel Jewish Identity and the Challenges of Today.* (BJEC: Montreal, 2006)

Name: _____ Date: _____

Definitions of Zionism

Rank every statement:
A – I strongly agree and this is very important to me
B – I agree and this is important to me
C – I somewhat agree and this is somewhat important to me
D – I somewhat disagree and this is somewhat unimportant to me
E – I strongly disagree and this is not very important to me

___ The Jews are a nation like the French or the Germans.

___ The Jews are a religious group like Muslims or Christians.

___ All Jews should live in Israel.

___ Jewish life in the Diaspora is vital to the continuation of the Jewish people.

___ Jewish life in the Diaspora can never be fully safe or satisfying.

___ Self-determination is the basic right of all peoples.

___ The Jewish claim for national independence is based on Divine promise as recorded in the Torah.

___ The Jewish people have an absolute and singular right to the Land of Israel as their national homeland.

___ The Land of Israel is the national homeland of both the Jewish and the Palestinian Arab people.

___ The State of Israel should be a model of Western liberal democracy.

___ The Torah is the national constitution of the Jewish people and should be the national constitution of the State of Israel.

___ The State of Israel belongs to the entire Jewish people.

___ The State of Israel belongs to the citizens of the State.

___ Israel is primarily a refuge for Jews fleeing oppression and a response to anti-Semitism.

___ Israel is primarily a creative expression of the Jewish people's will to be an independent community.

___ All citizens of the State of Israel, regardless of religion or national-cultural identity, should share the same rights and privileges.

___ Zionism demands personal fulfillment through Aliyah.

___ Any support of Israel is Zionism.

___ Zionism does not end with Aliyah, but continues through personal work to create a better society in Israel.

___ A person living in Israel has to volunteer for National Service to be considered a Zionist.

Name:_____ Date:_____

University of Michigan to Host 'Zionism is Racism' Conference.

Michael Freund, *The Jerusalem Post*

The University of Michigan at Ann Arbor is slated to play host to a national student conference late next week, one of whose "guiding principles" is that it "condemns the racism and discrimination inherent in Zionism", the *Jerusalem Post* has learned.

The Second National Student Conference on the Palestine Solidarity Movement, which is scheduled to begin on October 12, is being sponsored by pro-Palestinian and socialist groups. It aims to promote an end to U.S. aid to Israel and to encourage divestment by universities and corporations from the Jewish State.

In the conference's promotional material, organisers refer to "Apartheid Israel", and refuse to condemn Palestinian terrorism, stating, "As a solidarity movement, it is not our place to dictate the strategies or tactics adopted by the Palestinian people in their struggle for liberation."

In addition to asserting, "racism" is "inherent to Zionism", the organisers call for "the right of return and repatriation for all "Palestinian refugees" as well as "an end to the Israeli system of apartheid and discrimination."

Panelists at the conference include Dr. Sami Al-Arian, a former professor at the University of South Florida who was fired after reports surfaced linking him to Middle Eastern terrorist groups such as Al-Qaeda and Islamic Jihad.

A similar conference on divestment, held earlier this year at Berkeley, caused an uproar among American academics, leading Harvard President Lawrence Summers to criticize the divestment scheme as "anti-Semitic."

In a statement issued last week, University of Michigan President Mary Coleman appeared to distance the school from the conference, stating, "The agenda of the conference represents the views of the organisers and not the University of Michigan." She added that the University had no intention of divesting from Israel. "I do not support this divestment," she said, adding, "As a matter of University policy, we do not believe political interests should govern our investment decisions."

Questions:

1. What would you do if you were a Jewish student at the University of Michigan?
2. Write a letter to the Jerusalem Post and /or the school newspaper with your reaction to this article.

Name: _____ Date: _____

Violence at Concordia University

Sara Ahronheim

Dear Friends and Family,

This morning my friends and I set out to Concordia University, in the heart of downtown Montreal, to hear Benjamin Netanyahu (Prime Minister of Israel) speak. Many articles were featured in the Montreal papers leading up to today's speech, warning of protest action. I had a good idea of what we would face as we approached Concordia, but I could never have predicted what actually happened once we were there.

To enter the building we had to make a giant circle around it, to get to the supposedly "safe" entrance. We had to walk right through a volatile protest of hundreds of Palestinians and their supporters in keffiyehs, with flags, screaming vitriolic hate. Once having run this gauntlet, we waited patiently outside the Bishop Street entrance, held back at the gate by security and police. After about an hour they started admitting us inside, but it was too late because a huge group of Palestinian 'demonstrators' had appeared in our midst. I was fortunately right at the entrance, and as dozens of violent protesters pushed their way to the front, I tried to get through. Right next to me appeared the ringleader, who tried to push his way in. The cop in front of me punched him in the face while pulling me through the gate at the same time. I rested against the wall and watched as at least a hundred (I think) red-and-green coloured protesters attacked the barriers and tried to get in. Riot cops appeared, dozens of them, and went to the gate as a few others and I were herded into the building.

There was yelling and chanting, drumming and fighting going on outside the doors, with hundreds of our people stuck behind the gate being abused by hundreds of violent demonstrators. A few of us were waiting after the metal detectors for our friends to come through, when all of a sudden we heard loud chanting and yelling INSIDE the building. The riot cops came storming in and up the stairs beside us, and we began hearing fighting, crashing, yelling, punching. Chaos broke out and riot cops made us run for the door to the auditorium – I thought we were going to get killed, I swear. It was the scariest feeling, because I knew that these people wanted to hurt me and anyone who supports Israel or is Jewish.

Once inside the auditorium, we were told to be patient, as more people would drift in from the insanity outside. We waited inside for three hours, as the commotion

continued on next page

outside grew increasingly loud. We could hear chanting and yelling, and the protesters began trashing the university building. The police tear-gassed and pepper sprayed the entire building and outside, and we began to feel the effects if we stood too near the doors. After hours of waiting, and bomb searches by RCMP sniffer dogs, we were informed that Bibi Netanyahu could not speak after all – too much danger to him and to us. This was an incredible disappointment and we were naturally upset.

We however managed to maintain a kind of composure and instead of fighting, the 650 of us inside began to sing Hatikvah, the national anthem of the State of Israel. We sang peace chants and then just waited to be let out, in groups of 10, escorted by police.

The scene as we exited was disgusting. Benches were overturned, papers and garbage streaked across the hallways, and broken windows. We were shoved outside directly into a HUGE Palestinian riot, where some of our people were apparently attacked. The cops did nothing. We stood on one side of the barrier, while they stood on the other, and we faced off. On our side, we sang and danced and celebrated being free and Jewish. On their side, they threw bottles at people's heads, screamed hatred, and tried to break the barriers down to hurt us. They started tossing pennies and coins at us – one of the oldest ways to taunt Jews by saying we're all 'money-grubbing'. While we sang Hatikvah arm in arm, they spat at us. Finally we decided to disperse and leave them to their hatred.

Today was a sick and sorrowful day not only for the Jewish students and community of Montreal, but for Jews everywhere, the city of Montreal and Canada. Today a man was gagged and not allowed to express an opinion; today hundreds of people were denied the opportunity to listen to him speak. Today a riot broke forth on our peaceful streets, and today no police managed to restrain hate. Today Montreal Jews were made to feel afraid for our lives, and today Jewish students were threatened in our own home. If we cannot express ourselves here in Canada, champion of free speech and human rights, where on earth can we do so? If we cannot feel safe in our own cities where we have grown up and thrived, where are we to go?

I can answer my own question with what many of us already know – Israel is our place. She is our homeland, and opens her arms to us, willing to protect us at all costs. The Jewish people need Israel, and she needs us. Even so, we must voice our distaste at the violence, which occurred in Montreal today.

We must all take our own individual stands against this fascism, by which freedom of speech was denied. What happened today in my city cannot be condoned or allowed to repeat. We must act. So I am sending you this entire long letter, with my own personal feelings and an eyewitness account.

WORKSHEET #3

> *Please do what you can to see that this message is spread to anyone you can think of – from friends to work associates, to politicians, and from Jews to non-Jews alike. We have a chance to fix these wrongs, but only if we take action and don't sit back as passive observers. We say NEVER AGAIN, but unless we protest these attacks on our freedoms, it is fruitless to put up that chant. Last but certainly not least, a personal lament on our situation: today I saw raw hatred, and it cut me to the core.*
>
> *I have never feared for my life as I did today. I have never feared for our free society the way I do today. I wish beyond anything that we can one day fix the agonizing rifts between our peoples, and erase the hate from our and their hearts alike. It is most important for you to know what really happened here today, and it is vital that you see this side of the story.*

Questions:

1. What are your feelings about this article?
2. How do you think you would react to the violence at Concordia University?

"How easy it should be...to understand and support

the right of the Jewish people to live

in the ancient Land of Israel.

All men of good will exult in the fulfillment of G-d's promise that His

people should return in joy to rebuild

their plundered land.

This is Zionism, nothing more, nothing less."

(Martin Luther King Jr., 1967)

The Historical Connection: "A Link in the Chain"

MISCONCEPTION: "The first inhabitants of Palestine were the Canaanite Arabs." (2nd Grade Palestinian Authority textbook entitled, "National Education" – deals with the "history of Palestine.")

REALITY: The Jews have had a continuous connection to the Land of Israel for over three millennia. "Palestine" was the name given by the Romans to the Province of Judæa only from the second century CE. Canaanites were the native inhabitants (2nd Millennium BCE) and the Arab conquest of Byzantine-controlled Palestine was in the 7th century CE. The whole statement, therefore, is anachronistic.

The Historical Connection

Objectives

- Understand our connection to Israel
- Relate the 4,000 years of Jewish history to the tie with the Land of Israel
- Comprehend the relevance today of being a "link in the chain of (Jewish) existence and Israel's independence"

A: Introduction and Motivation

1. Remind students: "In the last unit we worked on defining Zionism in the twenty-first century. This was an important exercise to complete before we examine the phenomena of Arab violence and anti-Israel incitement on campus. However, it is not enough to just react. In order to "walk tall," defend, advocate for and promote Israel, we need to be armed with knowledge. With knowledge will come pride and confidence. In this unit we will examine our historical, religious and cultural connections to Israel and why it is important to be aware of these links."

2. Hand each pair of students Worksheet #1, ("Incitement and Propaganda against Israel and Zionism"). Have the students read it and then ask: "These are statements from Palestinian Authority children's textbooks, media sources and Yassir Arafat himself. How do they make you feel as a Jew and as a Zionist? Do you know how to respond?" We need to know our own history.

3. On a different note, ask the students: "In your opinion, which is the Jewish holiday that most effectively captures Jewish history and the Jewish experience throughout the ages?"

(This holiday is one in which one's extended family sits down and celebrates together). The answer should be Pesach, as will be explained

TUVIA

and emphasised below. Allow students the freedom to suggest any holiday and have them give reasons for their choices.

4. Inform the students that they will learn about a modern Jewish hero and hear his opinion regarding this same question.

5. "Yoni" – Tell Entebbe story synopsis;
   - Air France plane flies Sunday, June 27, 1976 (Tel Aviv–Athens–Paris).
   - Plane is hijacked in Athens by PFLP and flown to Entebbe airport in Uganda (Idi Amin)
   - "Selektzia" – 103 Jewish passengers held hostage.
   - "Operation (Thunderbolt) Yoni." (Israeli commandoes fly 2,500 miles to Uganda and rescue hostages.)
   - The single Israeli military fatality: Yonatan Netanyahu, the commander.

6. Suggestion: have the students watch the film "Follow Me, The Yoni Netanyahu Story" (2012)

7. After the students have seen the film, learned about Yoni and seen pictures of him, ask them how they felt about it and what the most moving aspect of the event was. What makes this a "miraculous" yet tragic episode (bittersweet)?

   By studying and talking about Yoni, we are actually helping to keep his memory alive. Look at a letter he wrote to his girlfriend not long before he was killed.

8. Distribute Worksheet #2, (Yoni's Letter). Have students read the letter and discuss the following points in groups of four:

   - Is this a typical love letter?
   - What is strange about it?
   - What is Yoni's favorite holiday? Why?
   - How can a Seder in a battle zone be as nice as one at home?
   - What does Yoni mean by "past?"
   - What do you mean by "past?"
   - What does it mean to be a "link in the chain of Jewish history?"

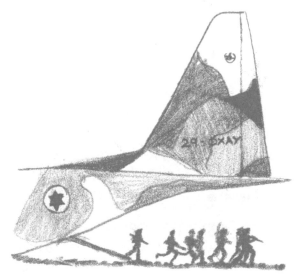

TUVIA

B. Introduction to Jewish History

1. Draw a line on the board with a "o" in the middle and ask the students to help you fill it in with Jewish dates they know. The time-line will probably end up looking something like this:

━ 586 ━━ 0 ━ 70 ━━━━ 1492 ━━━━━ 1939 ━━━━ 1948 ━ 1967 ━ 1973 ━ 1982 ━

After analyzing the dates, students will notice that there is a common theme; all the dates usually relate to negative events in Jewish history – destruction, death, expulsion etc. It is time to redefine the way we look at our history. Ask: "Is this all there is to Jewish history?" Let students try to answer as best as they can.

2. Transmit to the students the following critical message: "We need to comprehend that along with all the darkness and misery there is also light and joy. We need to restore pride and awe in our history. We need to realise that it's not a burden to be a Jew, but rather a privilege." To illustrate this point, explain how each of these dates had positive, wonderful and sometimes long precedents. Give examples.

(The Temples were not just destroyed in 586 BCE and 70 CE; they were built in c. 940 BCE and c. 536 BCE and stood for a millennium. The Jews were not just exiled from Spain in 1492; they lived there since Second Temple times and rose to levels of tremendous crea-

tivity and vitality. The same is true of the Jews of Eastern and Western Europe. Israel's history is not just one long war but also periods of remarkable scientific, agricultural, cultural and medical achievements, not to mention the unparalleled success of immigrant absorption).

3. Ask the students to discuss: "How did the Jews survive despite so much suffering and without physical possession of a homeland for many centuries?" Hand out Worksheet #3, ("Concerning the Jews", by Mark Twain).

4. Discuss: What are the ingredients of Jewish survival? How would you answer this? Write students' answers on the board. Divide the students' answers into the following three categories:
    *   Tradition (*Torat Yisrael*)
    *   People/Family (*Am Yisrael*)
    *   Land of Israel (*Eretz Yisrael*)

Identify the above as the 'secrets' of Jewish survival. Expand on these three points. Ask whether they are still relevant today.

C. Conclusion:

1. Ask students to share what they learned in this unit. What touched them the most?

2. Remind students that Jewish history is not all pain and suffering but also beauty and joy.

3. You can add the following: As a sixteen year old Yoni penned what were to be the guiding principals of his life:

TUVIA

> "...man does not live forever, and he should put the days of his life to the best possible use. He should try to live life to its fullest...I must feel certain that not only the moment of my death shall I be able to account for the time I've lived; I ought to be ready at every moment of my life to confront myself and say – This is what I've done."

Yoni saw himself as a "link in the chain of Jewish history" and as an heir to an ancient legacy – in a sense so are we all! To understand who we are today, we must begin by searching in our past. "Know from where you came and to where you are going." (Mishna)

"Know from where you came
and to where you are going"

(Mishna: Avot)

"צֵא מֵאַיִן בָּאתָ
וּלְאָן אַתָּה הוֹלֵךְ"

(מִשְׁנָה: אָבוֹת)

15

Name:_____ Date:_____

Incitement and Propaganda Against Israel and Zionism

"Abraham was not a Jew ... The Jews never lived in ancient Israel...

There never was a Jewish Temple in Jerusalem...

Jews never had any connection to Jerusalem...

That is not the Western Wall at all, but a Muslim shrine."

Unfortunately, these quotations represent mainstream Palestinian opinions, not an extremist fringe. They are respectively taken from a Palestinian-Arab historian named Jarid al-Kidwa, Palestinian television, the Palestinian Authority's Ministry of Information, and finally from the late Arafat himself (*Why I am a Zionist*, Troy 165).

The following text is taken from a 2nd grade textbook entitled, "National Education"* which deals with the "history of Palestine." It states:

"The first inhabitants of Palestine were the Canaanite Arabs."

Questions:
1. What is problematic about this declaration?
2. Can you identify the anachronisms?

 This picture is from a 7th grade textbook entitled, "Mathematics." It portrays a map of "Palestine" showing the territory as one single geographical entity, mentioning only "Palestinian" towns (Jerusalem, Gaza, Nablus [Shechem], Hebron). No mention is made of the name Israel or Israeli towns, which were established by the Zionist movement. (For instance, where is Tel Aviv?)

Questions:
1. How does this make you feel?
2. How do you think it is possible to counter this type of education?

_____

* Erlich Reuven (ed), Incitement and Propaganda against Israel and Zionism in the educational system of the Palestinian Authority and the alternative Islamic educational system identified with the Hamas. (Intelligence and Terrorism Information Center for Special Studies: Israel, June 2002)

WORKSHEET #2

Name: _____   Date: _____

Letter of Yonatan Netanyahu *

TUVIA

March 25, 1975

My Dearest Bruria,

Tomorrow is Passover.

I have always thought it is the most wonderful of all our holidays. It is an ancient celebration of freedom – a thousands-of-years-old liberty. When I sail back over the seas of our history, I pass through long years of suffering, oppression, of massacres, of ghettos, of banishments, of humiliation; many years that, in a historical perspective seem devoid of any ray of light-yet it isn't so. The fact that the idea of freedom remained, that hope persisted, that the flame of liberty continued to burn through the observance of this ancient festival, is to me testimony of the striving for freedom and idea of freedom in Israel.

In this search through our past we come upon other periods-of tranquility and liberty, when we were the people of the Land as well as the people of the Book. Yet even then, Passover was celebrated with the same ardour, for freedom is precious and its remembrance long.

And there were other periods of transition from bondage to liberty, periods of rising and revolt – and it is of those that Passover reminds me most of all. When I say Passover – the Feast of Freedom – I think at once of the Hasmoneans and the Bar-Kochwah revolt and the Exodus and Joshua's conquest of the land…

Last year I celebrated Seder with my men in a big tent near a Tel in a Syrian enclave that was being shelled, and that too, was a wonderful Seder in its way. My yearning for the past mingles with my longing for you, and because of you I find myself in my past. And find the time and desire to reminisce in order to share my life with you. Yet by "past" I mean not only my own past, but also the way in which I see myself as an inseparable part, a link in the chain of existence and Israel's independence.

Love,

Yoni

Questions:

1. Is this a typical love letter? What is strange about it?
2. What is Yoni's favorite holiday? Why?
3. How can a Seder in a battle zone be as nice as one at home?
4. What do you think it means to be a "link in the chain of Jewish history?"

_____

* Netanyahu, Jonathan, *The Letters of Jonathan Netanyahu*. (Gefen: Israel: 2001)

WORKSHEET #3

Name:_____ Date:_____

Mark Twain "Concerning the Jews"
(Harper's Magazine for March, 1898)

TUVIA

"If the statistics are right, the Jews constitute but one percent of the human race. It suggests a nebulous dim puff of stardust lost in the blaze of the Milky Way. Properly the Jew ought hardly to be heard of; but he is heard of, has always been heard of. He is as prominent on the planet as any other people, and his commercial importance is extravagantly out of proportion to the smallness of his bulk. His contributions to the world's list of great names in literature, science, art, music, finance, medicine, and abstruse learning are also away out of proportion to the weakness of his numbers. He has made a marvelous fight in this world, in all the ages; and has done it with his hands tied behind him. He could be vain of himself, and be excused for it. The Egyptian, the Babylonian, and the Persian rose, filled the planet with sound and splendor, then faded to dream-stuff and passed away; the Greek and the Roman followed, and made a vast noise, and they are gone; other peoples have sprung up and held their torch high for a time, but it burned out, and they sit in twilight now, or have vanished. The Jew saw them all, beat them all, and is now what he always was, exhibiting no decadence, no infirmities of age, no weakening of his parts, no slowing of his energies, no dulling of his alert and aggressive mind. All things are mortal but the Jew; all other forces pass, but he remains…

What is the secret of his immortality?"

Question:
What, in your opinion, is the secret of Jewish immortality?

The Religious Connection: "My Heart is in the East."

MISCONCEPTION: "Judaism, in its character as a religion, is not a nationality with an independent existence, likewise the Jews are not one people…" (Palestinian National Covenant, Article 20).

REALITY: Jews are a nation defined by their religion. This concept is unique in today's world. However, it was common in the ancient world. The Land of Israel is an integral part of the Jewish faith. It is the hub around which the Jewish religion revolves. Judaism without Israel is like a body without a heart.

The Religious Connection

Objectives:

- Understand the importance of the Land of Israel to the Jewish faith.
- Comprehend how the "yearning for Zion" is what helped keep the Jewish faith alive for almost two stateless millennia.
- Conduct a brief survey of major religious precepts and customs that highlight the relevancy of Israel in Jewish liturgy and practice.

A: Introduction and Motivation:

1. Remind the students that in the last unit, "The Historical Connection – The Link in the Chain," we offered a three-part answer to the secret of Jewish survival (even though according to logic, Judaism should have vanished): tradition (*Torat Yisrael*), people/family (*Am Yisrael*) and land (*Eretz Yisrael*). All three of these answers coalesce in the form of the Jewish religion.

2. Ask the students what Jewish practices they can think of that emphasise: the centrality of Israel; the importance of Israel; and, the yearning for Zion.

3. Zionism didn't start in 1897 at Basle. It has been an inseparable part of Judaism since inception. After the destruction of the Second Temple, the Rabbis infused "proto-Zionism" into Judaism.

   > "The consciousness of living in exile was common to Jews throughout the world. It explains why Zionism, a small political movement at its inception, could grow within half a century, to be the largest and most unifying movement in Jewish life." *
   >
   > (Rabbi Joseph Telushkin)

   Jews conclude both the holiest day of the year, "Yom Kippur," and the most celebrated family festival, "Pesach," with the invocation: "Next year in Jerusalem!" (See Worksheet #2)

TUVIA

---

* Telushkin, Joseph, *Jewish Literacy: The Most Important Things to Know About the Jewish Religion, Its People, and Its History*, (William Morrow and Company, Inc.: New York, 2008)

B. Israel in our faith and faith in Israel

Use the Siddur and the *Tanach* as a resource to identify Zionism in the following:

1. The Siddur: The *Amidah*, *Birkat Hamazon* (Grace After Meals) *Shema* (2nd paragraph) and the wedding ceremony (Tradition) – Worksheet #5

2. Festivals: Pesach/Succot/Shavuot/Chanukah (Family).

3. Customs: direction of ark, breaking a glass at the wedding, *Eicha*, leaving an area unpainted, etc. (Land)

4. Read through Worksheet #1. In addition answer questions on Worksheets #2, #3 and #4.

C. Conclusion:

"My heart is in the East, and I am in the furthermost West.

How then can I taste what I eat? And how can food be sweet to me?

While Zion is in fetters...and I am in Arab chains?"

"לִבִּי בְמִזְרָח וְאָנֹכִי בְּסוֹף מַעֲרָב.

אֵיךְ אֶטְעֲמָה אֵת אֲשֶׁר אֹכַל וְאֵיךְ יֶעֱרָב?

אֵיכָה אֲשַׁלֵּם נְדָרַי וָאֱסָרַי,

בְּעוֹד צִיּוֹן בְּחֶבֶל אֱדוֹם וַאֲנִי בְּכֶבֶל עֲרָב?"

– Yehuda Halevi (c. 1075–1141), Hebrew poet and religious thinker who lived in Muslim Spain

As the quote above illustrates, it is our constant yearning for Zion that has helped Judaism to sustain the belief that one day we would "go up to our land." No other people have managed to sustain a dream over such an extended period of time.

"My heart is in the East,
and I am in the furthermost West"

(Yehuda Halevi)

"לבי במזרח ואנכי בסוף מערב"

(יהודה הלוי)

Name:_____ Date:_____

Tanach: G-d's Promise of the Land

"וְנָתַתִּ֣י לְ֠ךָ וּלְזַרְעֲךָ֨ אַחֲרֶ֜יךָ אֵ֣ת | אֶ֣רֶץ מְגֻרֶ֗יךָ אֵ֚ת כָּל־אֶ֣רֶץ כְּנַ֔עַן לַאֲחֻזַּ֖ת עוֹלָ֑ם וְהָיִ֥יתִי לָהֶ֖ם לֵאלֹקִֽים:"

(בראשית פרק י"ז:ח)

"And I will give to you, and to your seed after you, the land in which you live, all the land of Canaan, for an everlasting possession; and I will be their G-d."

(Genesis, 17:8)

G-d repeated this oath to Isaac (Genesis 26: 3) and then to Jacob:

"וְאֶת־הָאָ֗רֶץ אֲשֶׁ֨ר נָתַ֧תִּי לְאַבְרָהָ֛ם וּלְיִצְחָ֖ק לְךָ֣ אֶתְּנֶ֑נָּה וּֽלְזַרְעֲךָ֥ אַחֲרֶ֖יךָ אֶתֵּ֥ן אֶת־הָאָֽרֶץ:"

(בראשית פרק ל"ה:י"ב)

"The land that I assigned to Abraham and Isaac, I assign to you, and to your heirs to come will I assign the land"

(Genesis 35:12)

Bible scholar Harry Orlinsky underscores Israel's centrality in the relationship between G-d and the Jews:

"Were it not for the Land that G-d promised on oath to Abraham and to Isaac and to Jacob and to their heirs forever, there would be no covenant. For be it noted that everything in the contract, all the blessings – economic, territorial, political, increase in population, and the like – all these would be forthcoming from G-d to Israel not in Abraham's native land in Mesopotamia...nor in Egypt, but in the Promised Land."

Even the fifth Commandment is linked to the land:

"כַּבֵּ֣ד אֶת־אָבִ֗יךָ וְאֶת־אִמֶּ֑ךָ לְמַ֙עַן֙ יַאֲרִכ֣וּן יָמֶ֔יךָ עַ֚ל הָֽאֲדָמָ֔ה אֲשֶׁר־ה' אֱלֹקֶ֖יךָ נֹתֵ֥ן לָֽךְ:"

(שמות כ:י"ב)

"Honour your father and mother, that you may long endure on the land that the L-rd your G-d is giving to you"

(Exodus 20:12).

continued on next page

WORKSHEET #1

The most extreme punishment with which the ancient Hebrews are threatened is captivity followed by exile from the land (see Hosea 9:3 and Amos 7:17). Significantly, the very prophets who threaten the Jews with this fate also promise that G-d will restore them to Israel (see Hosea 11:11 and Amos 9:11–15).

This was an unusual prophecy, given that no other people ever had been exiled *en masse* from its homeland and then restored. Indeed, a prophecy offered by Amos twenty-eight hundred years ago seems to foretell the Jews' late nineteenth and twentieth-century return to Zion, even emphasising Israel's agricultural revitalization:

"I will restore my people Israel.

They shall rebuild ruined cities and inhabit them;

They shall plant vineyards and drink their wine;

They shall till gardens and eat their fruits.

And I will plant them upon their soil,

Nevermore to be uprooted

From the soil I have given them

Said the L-rd your G-d."

(Amos 9:14–15)

"וְשַׁבְתִּי אֶת־שְׁבוּת עַמִּי יִשְׂרָאֵל

וּבָנוּ עָרִים נְשַׁמּוֹת וְיָשָׁבוּ

וְנָטְעוּ כְרָמִים וְשָׁתוּ אֶת־יֵינָם

וְעָשׂוּ גַנּוֹת וְאָכְלוּ אֶת־פְּרִיהֶם:

וּנְטַעְתִּים עַל־אַדְמָתָם

וְלֹא יִנָּתְשׁוּ עוֹד

מֵעַל אַדְמָתָם אֲשֶׁר נָתַתִּי לָהֶם

אָמַר ה' אֱלֹקֶיךָ:"

(עמוס ט:י"ד–ט"ו)

View from Mount Gilboa

Photo by Tuvia Book

Tanach: G-d's Promise of the Land *page 2 of 2*

Name: _____   Date: _____

Natan Sharansky: "Next year in Jerusalem"

"Next year in Jerusalem"   "לְשָׁנָה הַבָּאָה בִּירוּשָׁלָיִם"

NATAN (ANATOLY) SHARANSKY (1948–) was born in Ukraine. In 1973, he applied for an exit visa to Israel but was denied for "security" reasons. He continued to engage in underground Zionist activities until his arrest by the Soviet authorities in 1977 on trumped-up charges of treason and espionage. Sharansky was found guilty in 1978 and sentenced to 13 years imprisonment. An international campaign calling for Sharansky's release was waged by his wife Avital, in conjunction with organizations around the world, culminating in his release on February 11, 1986. He arrived in Israel that same night.

He has continued to lead human rights efforts both through his writings as well as public activities since his release. Following his service as a Member of Knesset and Government Minister, Sharansky was sworn in as Chairman of the Jewish Agency for Israel in 2008.

Excerpts from Anatoly Sharansky's final statement in the Soviet court presented before being sentenced on trumped-up charges for treason and espionage, July 14, 1978

Sharansky addressed his first remarks to those who were not in the courtroom, his wife Avital who emigrated to Israel, and the Jewish people:

"During my interrogation the chief investigators threatened me that I might be executed by a firing squad, or imprisoned for at least fifteen years. But if I agreed to cooperate with the investigation for the purpose of destroying the Jewish emigration movement, they promised me freedom and a quick reunion with my wife."

"Five years ago, I submitted my application for exit to Israel. Now I am further than ever from my dream. It would seem to be cause for regret. But it is absolutely the other way around. I am happy. I am happy that I lived honorably, at peace with my conscience. I never compromised my soul, even under the threat of death…"

"For more that two thousand years the Jewish people, my people, have been dispersed. But wherever they are, wherever Jews are found, every year they have repeated,' Next year in Jerusalem.' Now, when I am further than ever from my people, from Avital, facing many arduous years of imprisonment, I say, turning to my people, my Avital, 'Next year in Jerusalem.'"

"Now I turn to you, the court, who were required to confirm a predetermined sentence: To you I have nothing to say." *

Questions:

1. What Jewish customs remind us of our attachment to Jerusalem?
2. How do you think Sharansky managed to survive mentally in the Soviet Gulag system?
3. What was your reaction to Sharansky's speech?

———————————
* Natan Sharansky, *Fear no Evil*, (Public Affairs: USA, 1998)

Name:_____   Date:_____

Talmud: Mitzvah (Commandment) of Living in Israel

That the Rabbis were willing to permit divorce when a couple disagreed over whether to live in Israel demonstrates not a callous disregard for the sacredness of marriage (indeed, Jewish law is known for its extraordinary regard for family life), but an even greater commitment to Jewish settlement in the land of Israel.

ת"ר: הוא אומר לעלות, והיא אומרת שלא לעלות – כופין אותה לעלות, ואם לאו – תצא בלא
כתובה, היא אומרת לעלות, והוא אומר שלא לעלות – כופין אותו לעלות, ואם לאו – יוציא
ויתן כתובה, היא אומרת לצאת, והוא אומר שלא לצאת – כופין אותה שלא לצאת, ואם לאו –
תצא בלא כתובה; הוא אומר לצאת, והיא אומרת שלא לצאת – כופין אותו שלא לצאת, ואם
לאו – יוציא ויתן כתובה.

(תלמוד בבלי: מסכת כתובות, ק"י, עמוד ב)

Mishna: *One may compel his entire household to go up with him to the Land of Israel, but none may be compelled to leave it. All of one's household may be compelled to go up to Jerusalem [from any other part of Israel], but none may be compelled to leave it.*

Gemara: *Our Rabbis taught: If the husband desires to go to live in Israel and his wife refuses, she may be pressured to go with him, and if she refuses, she may be divorced without being given the financial settlement promised in her Ketuba (marriage contract). If she desires to go live in Israel and if he does not consent, he is pressured to go with her, and if he refuses, he must divorce her and pay her the financial settlement promised in her Ketuba.*

(Babylonian Talmud, Ketubot 110b)

Affiliated, and especially observant, Diaspora Jews usually prefer to live in largely Jewish neighborhoods. However, the Talmud decrees:

ת"ר: לעולם ידור אדם בא"י אפי' בעיר שרובה עובדי כוכבים, ואל ידור בחו"ל
אפילו בעיר שרובה ישראל

(תלמוד בבלי: מסכת כתובות, ק"י, עמוד ב)

One should always live in the land of Israel, even in a city the majority of whose residents are not Jews, rather than live outside the land, even in a city the majority of whose residents are Jews.

(Babylonian Talmud, Ketubot 110b)

Questions:
1. What do the preceding Talmudic texts teach us about our connection to the Land of Israel? Do you agree with the texts?
2. In light of the above texts, why do some observant Jews live outside Israel?

WORKSHEET #4

Name: _____ Date: _____

Rashi on Genesis 1:1

RASHI (1040–1105), the eleventh-century French Biblical exegete, whose Torah commentary is still studied in traditional Jewish schools, also emphasises Israel's centrality. Writing a thousand years after the Jews were exiled from Israel, he begins his commentary on Genesis 1:1 ("In the beginning G-d created the heaven and the earth") with immediate reference to Israel, and the implicit expectation that the Jews would someday return:

"In the beginning" – *Rabbi Isaac states: Strictly speaking, the Torah should have commenced with the verse: "This month shall be to you the beginning of months" (Exodus 12:2), which is the very first commandment given to Israel. (Note: The commandment obligates the sanctifying of each month.) Why then, did the Torah begin with the account of the creation? To illustrate that G-d the Creator owns the whole world. So, if the peoples of the world shall say to Israel: "You are robbers in conquering the territory of the seven Canaanite nations," Israel can answer them: " All the earth belongs to G-d – He created it, so He can give it to whomsoever He wills. When he wished, He gave it to them, then when He wished, He took it away from them and gave it to us."*

(Rashi on Genesis 1:1)

בראשית – אמר רבי יצחק
לא היה צריך להתחיל [את]
התורה אלא שהיא מצוה
ראשונה שנצטוו [בה] ישראל,
ומה טעם פתח בבראשית,
משום (תהלים קי"א:ו) כח
מעשיו הגיד לעמו לתת להם
נחלת גוים, שאם יאמרו
אומות העולם לישראל
לסטים אתם, שכבשתם
ארצות שבעה גוים, הם
אומרים להם כל הארץ הוא
בראה ונתנה לאשר ישר
בעיניו, ברצונו נתנה להם
וברצונו נטלה מהם ונתנה לנו:
(רש"י בראשית, פרק א:א)

Question:
What do you think of Rashi's explanation?

Name: _____ Date: _____

Siddur

Look up the translation of the following sentences from our everyday prayers. The theme of Zionism that runs through them is clearly apparent.

שמע:

לְמַעַן יִרְבּוּ יְמֵיכֶם וִימֵי בְנֵיכֶם עַל הָאֲדָמָה אֲשֶׁר נִשְׁבַּע ה' לַאֲבֹתֵיכֶם לָתֵת לָהֶם כִּימֵי הַשָּׁמַיִם עַל־הָאָרֶץ:

עמידה:

תְּקַע בְּשׁוֹפָר גָּדוֹל לְחֵרוּתֵנוּ. וְשָׂא נֵס לְקַבֵּץ גָּלֻיּוֹתֵינוּ. וְקַבְּצֵנוּ יַחַד מֵאַרְבַּע כַּנְפוֹת הָאָרֶץ.

וְלִירוּשָׁלַיִם עִירְךָ בְּרַחֲמִים תָּשׁוּב. וְתִשְׁכֹּן בְּתוֹכָהּ כַּאֲשֶׁר דִּבַּרְתָּ. וּבְנֵה אוֹתָהּ בְּקָרוֹב בְּיָמֵינוּ בִּנְיַן עוֹלָם. וְכִסֵּא דָוִד מְהֵרָה לְתוֹכָהּ תָּכִין.

אֶת־צֶמַח דָּוִד עַבְדְּךָ מְהֵרָה תַצְמִיחַ וְקַרְנוֹ תָּרוּם בִּישׁוּעָתֶךָ כִּי לִישׁוּעָתְךָ קִוִּינוּ כָּל־הַיּוֹם.

וְתֶחֱזֶינָה עֵינֵינוּ בְּשׁוּבְךָ לְצִיּוֹן בְּרַחֲמִים.

ברכת המזון:

נוֹדֶה לְךָ ה' אֱלֹקֵינוּ עַל שֶׁהִנְחַלְתָּ לַאֲבוֹתֵינוּ, אֶרֶץ חֶמְדָּה טוֹבָה וּרְחָבָה

כַּכָּתוּב, וְאָכַלְתָּ וְשָׂבָעְתָּ וּבֵרַכְתָּ אֶת־ה' אֱלֹקֶיךָ עַל־הָאָרֶץ הַטֹּבָה אֲשֶׁר נָתַן־לָךְ:

רַחֵם נָא ה' אֱלֹקֵינוּ, עַל יִשְׂרָאֵל עַמֶּךָ, וְעַל יְרוּשָׁלַיִם עִירֶךָ, וְעַל צִיּוֹן מִשְׁכַּן כְּבוֹדֶךָ, וְעַל מַלְכוּת בֵּית דָּוִד מְשִׁיחֶךָ, וְעַל הַבַּיִת הַגָּדוֹל וְהַקָּדוֹשׁ שֶׁנִּקְרָא שִׁמְךָ עָלָיו.

וּבְנֵה יְרוּשָׁלַיִם עִיר הַקֹּדֶשׁ בִּמְהֵרָה בְיָמֵינוּ.

הָרַחֲמָן, הוּא יִשְׁבּוֹר עֻלֵּנוּ מֵעַל צַוָּארֵנוּ וְהוּא יוֹלִיכֵנוּ קוֹמְמִיּוּת לְאַרְצֵנוּ.

"Thus said the L-rd G-d:

...you, O mountains of Israel, shall yield your produce

and bear your fruit for My people Israel, for their return is near. For I

will care for you: I will turn to you,

and you shall be tilled and sown.

I will settle a large population on you, the whole House of Israel; the

towns shall be resettled, and the ruined cities rebuilt."

(Ezekiel, 36)

Streams of Zionism

MISCONCEPTION: Zionism is a monolithic movement that brokers no argument.

REALITY: Zionism is multi-faceted and dynamic, with factions on the left and right, religious and secular, and is a living movement whose uniting link is love for Israel.

Objectives:

- Understand the differing philosophies that are integral to modern Zionism.
- Learn about the personalities that have shaped the different streams within the Zionist movement.
- Comprehend how multi-faceted and lively Zionism is.

A: Introduction and Motivation:

1. In 1897, the Jewish world was electrified by the news of the first Zionist Congress in Basel, Switzerland. The old-new idea of Zionism ignited a wave of enthusiasm throughout the Jewish world when Theodor Herzl gave it a "new" face.

2. We have all heard the expression, "two Jews, three opinions." Zionism was no exception. There were many divergent philosophies within the movement, both politically and religiously.

3. There was, however, a common thread that united the various factions. They ultimately had the same goal: "To establish a Jewish State / homeland in the Land of Israel."

TUVIA

B: Left, Right, Religious and Secular

In order to make this complex topic of differing Zionist philosophies more interactive and engaging, this unit will focus on an art component entitled: "Zionist Conference Project."

1. Read Worksheet #1 entitled: "The Basel Program". Remind the students how revolutionary the concept was of a council of Jews advocating for a Jewish homeland in the Land of Israel almost two millennia after the Roman destruction of the Temple. Discuss the three questions at the foot of the worksheet.

2. Divide students into five equal groups. Each group is assigned to study a different philosophy of Zionism (Worksheets #2–6). They then work together to present their topic to the other students. The presentations should include the following components:

   - A brief summary of the movement and its leader
   - An artistic "propaganda" poster capturing the movement's ideology
   - An original song
   - Short dramatic skit

3. At the conclusion of the "Zionist Conference," students should fill a chart similar to the one at the foot of this page.

4. At the end of the worksheets, there are engaging questions that should lead to group discussion of the differing movements' ideological statements. This method of "peer teaching" is very effective.

5. The educator should "wrap up" the conference by succinctly summarising the five main ideologies of classic Zionism.

Zionist Philosophy	Personality	Political Ideology
Political	Theodor Herzl (1860–1904)	
Cultural	Achad Ha'am (1856–1927)	
Labour	A.D. Gordon (1856–1922)	
Religious	Rav A.I. Kook (1865–1935)	
Revisionist	Ze'ev Jabotinsky (1880–1940)	

Conclusion:

It is important to emphasise the richness of Zionist thought and to stress that, despite its many disparate views, there was a common consensus: the Love of Zion (*Ahavat Zion*) in order to bring about:

> *"The hope of 2000 years, to be a free people in our land, the Land of Zion, Jerusalem."*
>
> (Hatikvah)

In our own generation, we need to recapture that passionate and emotional attachment to Israel.

"If you will it,
it is not a dream"

(Theodor Herzl)

"אם תרצו אין זו אגדה"

(בניאור אלס הרצל)

Name:_____ Date:_____

The Basel Program

Theodor Herzl called the First Zionist Congress a symbolic parliament for those who were sympathetic to the implementation of Zionist goals. Herzl had planned to hold the gathering in Munich, but due to local Jewish opposition he transferred the gathering to Basel, Switzerland. The Congress took place in the concert hall of the Basel Municipal Casino.

The First Zionist Congress opened on August 29, 1897, and was attended by some 204 participants from seventeen countries. Following a festive opening in which the representatives were expected to arrive in formal dress, tails and white tie, the Congress got down to the business at hand. The main items on the agenda were the presentation of Herzl's plans, the establishment of the World Zionist Organisation and the declaration of Zionist plans as formulated in the Basel Program (see below). Herzl was elected President of the Organisation and Max Nordau one of three Vice-Presidents.

"THE BASEL PROGRAM," 1897

This Program provided the guidelines for the work of the Zionist Organisation, from its foundation at the First Zionist Congress (August 1897) until the establishment of the State of Israel. It reads:

"Zionism seeks to secure for the Jewish People a publicly recognised, legally secured home (or homeland) in Palestine for the Jewish people." For the achievement of its purpose the Congress envisaged the following methods:

1. The encouragement of settling Palestine with Jewish agricultural workers, labourers and artisans;
2. The unification and organisation of all Jewry into local and general groups in accordance with the laws of their respective countries;
3. The strengthening of Jewish self-awareness and national consciousness;
4. The preparation for obtaining the consent of the various governments necessary for fulfilling the aim of Zionism.

Questions:
1. What are the strengths and weaknesses of this statement?
2. What would you have added or removed from the Program?
3. How would you compose a four-point program of action for Zionism in the twenty-first century?

Name:_____ Date:_____

Political Zionism

THEODOR HERZL (1860–1904) was the father of political Zionism and founder of the World Zionist Organisation. While serving as the Paris correspondent for a Viennese newspaper from 1890 to 1895, Herzl – an assimilated Jew of minimal Jewish commitment – was aroused by the increase of anti-Semitism in liberal France. The Dreyfus Case – the trial and the public demand for "Death to the Jew" – prompted Herzl to draw the conclusion that the only feasible solution to the Jewish question was a mass exodus of Jews from the countries of their torment and resettlement in a land of their own. He devoted the remainder of his tragically short life to the realisation of this goal.

TUVIA

SOURCE #1: *THE JEWISH STATE* (1896)

"The whole plan is essentially quite simple, as it must be if it is to be comprehensive to all. Let sovereignty be granted us over some portion of the globe adequate to meet our rightful national requirements; we will attend to the rest. To create a new State is neither ridiculous nor impossible… The governments of all countries scourged by anti-Semitism will be keenly interested in obtaining sovereignty for us. The plan, simple in design but complicated in execution, will be carried out by two agencies: the Society of Jews and the Jewish Company. The Jewish Company will carry out the scientific plan and political policies, which the Society of Jews will establish. The Jewish Company will be the liquidating agent for the business interest of departing Jews, and will organise trade and commerce in the new country.

The Society of Jews will treat with respect present authorities in the land, under sponsorship of the European powers, if they prove friendly to the plan. We could offer the present authorities enormous advantages, assume part of the public debt, and build new thoroughfares that we would also need, and do many other things. The very creation of the Jewish State would be beneficial to the neighboring lands, since the cultivation of a strip of land increases the value of its surrounding districts."

Questions:
1. Why did the success of the Zionists building up the economy and agriculture lead to increased Arab immigration?
2. Can you think of contemporary equivalents of "The Society of Jews" and "The Jewish Company"?
3. Herzl's plan was "essentially quite simple" – but was it realistic?

continued on next page

SOURCE #2: A SOLUTION TO THE JEWISH QUESTION (1896)

"We shall plant for our children in the same way as our fathers preserved the tradition for us. Our lives represent but a moment in the permanent duration of our people. This moment had its duties...In vain are we loyal patriots, in some places our loyalty running to extremes...In places where we have lived for centuries we are still cried down...In our land we do not mean to found a theocracy, but a tolerant modern civil state. We shall, however, rebuild the Temple in glorious remembrance of the faith of our fathers...Our flag should consist of seven stars on a white field...The white field symbolises our pure new life, the seven stars, the seven golden hours of a working day. For we shall march into the Promised Land carrying the badge of labour... The Society of Jews will be the nucleus of our public organisations... What form of constitution shall we have? I incline to an aristocratic republic...What language shall we speak? Every man can preserve the language in which his thoughts are at home...We can do nothing without the enthusiasm of our own nation...A wondrous generation of Jews will spring into existence. The Macabbean will rise again...We shall live at last, as free men, on our own soil, and die peacefully in our own home."

Questions:

1. What does this excerpt tell you about Herzl's personality and background?
2. Do you agree with the following statement: "In vain are we loyal patriots" Are Jews destined to be eternal outsiders?
3. Why did the secular Herzl want to rebuild the Temple?
4. Herzl describes his Jewish flag. How would you design a Jewish flag? What symbols would you incorporate?
5. Which parts of Herzl's closing sentence have become realities? Do you think that there is a chance of realising his dream expressed in the following sentence: "The Macabbean will rise again...We shall live at last, as free men, on our own soil, and die peacefully in our own home?"

Political Zionism *page 2 of 2*

Name: _____   Date: _____

Cultural Zionism

ASHER GINZBERG "ACHAD HA'AM" (1856–1927) was the doyen of cultural Zionism. He saw the need for a Jewish cultural and spiritual revival. Achad Ha'Am's concept of Zionism established him as a philosopher. It was founded upon an original explanation of reality and ideals. For many years he was opposed to political Zionism, advocating instead the establishment of a Jewish cultural center in Palestine. This, he hoped, would become a "center of emulation" for Jews dispersed all over the world, effectively raising their cultural standards and inspiring them to produce a genuine Jewish culture.

THE ZIONIST IDEA

"Judaism is, therefore, in a quandary; it can no longer tolerate the *Galut* (exile) form, which it had to take on in obedience to its will to live when it was exiled from its own country; but without that form, its life is in danger. So it seeks to return to its historic center, where it will be able to live a life developing in every natural way, to bring its powers into play in every department of human life, to broaden and perfect those national possessions which it has acquired up to now, and thus contribute to the common stock of humanity, unhampered activity of a people living by its own spirit. For this purpose Judaism can, for the present, content itself with very little. It does not need an independent state, but only the creation in its native land of conditions favourable to development, a good sized settlement of Jews working without hindrance in every branch of civilization, from agriculture to handicrafts and science and literature. This Jewish settlement, which will be gradual in its growth, will become in the course of time the center of the nation, wherein its spirit will find pure expression and develop in all its aspects to the highest degree of perfection of which it is capable. Then, from this center, the spirit of Judaism will radiate to the great circumference to all the communities of the Diaspora, to inspire them with new life and to preserve the overall unity of our people. When our national culture in Palestine has attained that level, we may be confident that it will produce men in the Land of Israel itself who will be able, at a favourable moment, to establish a State there, one which will be not merely a State of Jews, but a Jewish State.

This secret of our people's persistence is that at a very early period the Prophets taught it to

continued on next page

WORKSHEET #3

respect only the power of the spirit and not to worship material power. Therefore, unlike the other nations of antiquity, the Jewish people never reached the point of losing its self-respect in the face of more powerful enemies. As long as we remain faithful to this principle, our existence has a secure basis and we shall not lose our self-respect, for we are not spiritually inferior to any nation…"

Photo by Tuvia Book

"Living Hebrew: Notice Board in Jerusalem"

Questions:

1. Does Israel need a strong diaspora in order to survive or should all Jews live in Israel?
2. How could Achad Ha'am be considered a Zionist if he wrote, "Judaism…does not need an independent state?"
3. What were the major differences between Herzl's and Achad Ha'am's philosophies?
4. What do you think Achad Ha'am means by "the power of the spirit"?

Cultural Zionism *page 2 of 2*

Name:_____ Date:_____

Labour Zionism

TUVIA

A.D. GORDON (1856–1922) was the Grandfather of Labour Zionism. At the mature age of forty-seven, he decided to leave Russia and come to *Eretz Yisrael* and begin a life of agricultural labour, first in Petach-Tikvah, later in Rishon Le-Zion, and finally made his home in Degania, the first of the *kvutsot* (proto-kibbutzim). It should be remembered that Gordon had been a white-collar worker his whole life and had no experience with agricultural labour. However, he believed that physical effort on the land would bring about not only his personal redemption but also that of the Jewish people. He attributed to pioneer work a semi-religious status, arguing that it created an organic inter-relationship between the person, the land, and the culture. Gordon became the inspiration for an entire generation and for Labour Zionists who saw in his example an avenue towards personal and national fulfillment. Gordon died in 1922 and was buried in Degania where he had lived during his final years.

OUR TASK AHEAD (1920)

"The Jewish people have been completely cut off from nature and imprisoned within city walls for two thousand years. We have been accustomed to every form of life, except a life of labour done on our behalf and for its own sake. It will require the greatest effort of will for such a people to become normal again. We lack the principal ingredient for national life. We lack the habit of labour...for it is labour which binds a people to its soil and to its national culture, which in its turn is an outgrowth of the people's soil and the people's labour.

Now it is true that every people has many individuals who shun physical labour and try to live off the work of others...We Jews have developed an attitude of looking down on physical labour...but labour is the only force which binds man to the soil...it is the basic energy for the creation of national culture. This is what we do not have, but we are not aware of missing it. We are a people without a country, without a national living language, without a national culture. We seem to think that if we have no labour it does not matter, let Ivan, John, or Mustapha do the work, while we busy ourselves with producing a culture, with creating national values, and with enthroning absolute justice in the world.

As we now come to re-establish our path among the ways of living nations of the earth, we must make sure that we find the right path. We must create a new people, a human people, whose attitude toward other people is informed with the sense of human brotherhood and whose attitude toward nature, and all within it, is inspired by noble urges of life loving creativity. All the forces of our history, all the pain that has accumulated in our national soul, seem to impel us in that direction...we are engaged in a creative endeavour, the like of which is not to be found in the whole history of mankind: the rebirth and rehabilitation of a people that has been uprooted and scattered to the winds…

The center of our national work, the heart of our people, is here, in Palestine, even though we are but a small community in this country, for here is the mainspring of our life. Here, in this central spot, is hidden the vital force of our cause and its potential growth…What we seek to establish in Palestine is a new, recreated Jewish people, not a mere colony of Diaspora Jewry, not a continuation of Diaspora Jewish life in a new form. It is our aim to make Jewish Palestine the mother country of world Jewry, with Jewish communities in the Diaspora as its colonies, and not the reverse. We seek the rebirth of our national self, the manifestation of our loftiest spirit, and for that we must give our all."

Photo by Tuvia Book

"Aaron Works the Land"

Questions:

1. A.D. Gordon wrote, "We lack the principal ingredient for national life. We lack the habit of labour…for it is labour which binds a people to its soil and to its national culture." Is this still relevant today?

2. Today we let "Ivan, John, or Mustapha do the work." Does this mean that we have lost the way? Now that Jews don't do as much physical labour, is A.D. Gordon's vision dead?

Labour Zionism *page 2 of 2*

WORKSHEET #5

Name:_____ Date:_____

Religious Zionism

RABBI ABRAHAM ISAAC KOOK (1865–1935) was the spiritual figure-head of a religious national philosophy. Rabbi Kook was appointed the first Ashkenazi Chief Rabbi of pre-state Israel. He tried to broaden the outlook of the yeshivot to cope with modern ideas and train spiritual leaders. His mystical leanings helped him embrace even the non-religious pioneers and earned him the respect of the entire Zionist world. Rabbi Kook believed that the "secularist" Zionists were performing a religious mission, even if they were unaware of it. He saw them as fueled by sincere, altruistic motives, and not as heretics. Rabbi Kook set up his own yeshiva, which later became known as Mercaz Harav. He wrote many books on philosophy and halachah (Jewish law).

TUVIA

WRITINGS OF RABBI KOOK

"Only through their longing for the Land of Israel, will exilic Judaism receive its inherent qualities and essential characteristics. Yearning for Salvation, is the force that preserves Exilic Judaism, whereas the Judaism of the Land of Israel, is the very Salvation itself."

Orot, 1

"The secrets of Torah bring the redemption and return Israel to its land, for the Torah of Truth, with the strength of its inner logic, demands with its broadening the whole soul of the nation, and through it, the nation begins to feel the pain of Exile and how it is utterly impossible for its character to be actualized as long as it is oppressed upon foreign soil."

Orot, 64

"We experience exile and mediocrity because we do not proclaim the value and wisdom of the land of Israel. We have not rectified the sin of the biblical spies who slandered the land. And so we must do the opposite of what they did: we must tell and proclaim to the entire world the land's glory and its beauty, its holiness and its honor. Then, after all these praises, let us hope that we have expressed at least one ten-thousandth of the loveliness of that lovely land: the beauty of the light of its Torah, the exalted nature of the light of its wisdom, and the holy spirit that seethes within it. *Eretz Chafetz* (The land of our desire)."

Orot Kedusha

"Only in Israel's divinely determined homeland can the Torah achieve its full and vital purpose. Such is the correspondence in Israel between the concept of G-d and the national idea that the roots of the one are at all times discernible in the other. Many of the lapses of our national religious life which exist today are due to the unusual hardships we have expe-

continued on next page

rienced during the many years of exile. Being far from our homeland, we have slipped into complacency; being persecuted has warped our true nature. We did not have the advantage of breathing the holy and pure air of *Eretz Yisrael*. But now, with the great redemption taking place, the therapeutic quality of the Land of Israel will revive us and cure our ills."

"The purely righteous do not complain about evil, rather they add justice.

They do not complain about heresy, rather they add faith.

They do not complain about ignorance, rather they add wisdom."

Arpilei Tohar

"Just as the Temple was destroyed through baseless hatred (*Sinat Chinam*), it will only be rebuilt through baseless love (*Ahavat Chinam*)."

Photo by Tuvia Book

Yom Yerushalayim at the Kotel

Questions:
1. How far are we from realising Rabbi Kook's dream of "baseless love" (*ahavat chinam*) towards our fellow Jews? What can we do to foster this love despite our differences?
2. What do you think is meant by the "true nature" referred to by Rabbi Kook?
3. Do you agree that "Only in Israel's divinely determined homeland can the Torah achieve its full and vital purpose." If so, is it inconsistent for religious Zionists to live outside of Israel (*Chutz LaAretz*)?

Religious Zionism *page 2 of 2*

Name:_____ Date:_____

Revisionist Zionism

VLADIMIR ZE'EV JABOTINSKY (1880–1940) was the founder of Revisionist Zionism. He was a Russian-born Zionist leader who employed his great oratorical and analytical skills in the advocacy of political Zionism. Like Herzl, he regarded the Jewish question as preeminently the problem of anti-Semitism and Jewish suffering. Dissatisfied with the acquiescence of the World Zionist Organisation to what he believed to be unsatisfactory policies of the Palestine Mandatory administration, Jabotinsky resigned from the Zionist Executive in 1923. As an expression of his opposition to official Zionism, in 1925 in Paris he founded the World Union of Zionist Revisionists.

TUVIA

VLADIMIR ZE'EV JABOTINSKY
WHAT THE ZIONIST-REVISIONISTS WANT (1926)

"The first aim of Zionism is the creation of a Jewish majority on both sides of the Jordan River…Is it too late to preach a "modified Zionism" for the Arabs have already read Herzl's *The Jewish State* as well as an even more "dangerous" Zionist manifesto – the Bible? Furthermore, the concealment, and particularly the negation of our aims is politically dangerous… In order to create a solid Jewish majority within twenty-five years in western Palestine we need an average yearly immigration of 40,000 Jews. If we take the area east of the Jordan into consideration, then we will need from 50,000 to 60,000 Jewish immigrants annually… The opening up of the area east of the Jordan is the first and most important of the reforms [needed to ensure the absorption of mass Jewish immigration]. To be sure, Trans-Jordan is part of the territory of the mandate, but it was subsequently excluded from the Zionist realm of influence within the mandate. This is a practical and historical injustice. Historically, the area east of the Jordan was always considered to be an integral part of Jewish Palestine…How are these concessions [which we are demanding from the mandatory authority] to be obtained? Suffice it to give a very brief reply to this question: with the same means employed by Herzl, namely through the instruction, persuasion and organisation of public opinion among Jewry, the British and the entire civilized world. This is the sole meaning of the familiar slogan: "political offensive."…Zionism appeals to the entire Jewish people for help in the reconstuction of the Land of Israel. We call upon every Jew not only to give but to come and share the responsibility with us. But – and this must remain absolutely clear at all times – the extent of responsibility depends on what is given.

The first condition of a national state is a national majority. For a long time many Jews, including Zionists, were unwilling to understand this simple truth. They maintained that the crea-

continued on next page

tion of important positions in Palestine (colonies, cities, schools) was enough. According to them, a national life could be freely developed even though the majority of the population was to be Arabs. This is a vast mistake. History proves that any national position, however strong and important they may be, cannot be safeguarded as long as the nation, which built them, does not constitute a majority.

After attaining a majority in Palestine and being enabled to govern upon broadly democratic principles, we will have before us an even more important task: *Shivat Zion* (The Return to Zion). By this we mean the creation of conditions which would enable every Jew who is unwilling or unable to live in the Diaspora to settle in the Jewish State and earn his livelihood there. These would probably reach into the millions.

After this would come what is probably the most important task of all: to make Palestine the leading state of the civilized world, a country the customs and laws of which are to be followed by the whole universe. "From Zion the Torah shall come forth," signifies a "Torah" not merely in the religious sense. Zionism is a tremendous, overwhelmingly important task the boundaries of which our generation cannot as yet envisage. The first step, the deed without which there can be no Zionism, or a Jewish State, or a real Jewish nation, is the creation of a Jewish majority in Palestine on both sides of the Jordan.

First of all, however, the Jewish nation must build its state. This undertaking is so complicated and difficult that it demands the full strength of an entire generation; perhaps of even more than one generation. Jewish youth must, therefore, devote itself completely to this sole task; all other ideals, though they might be beautiful and humane, should influence us only in so far as they do not hinder the rebuilding of a Jewish State. When one of these ideals becomes (even indirectly) an obstacle on the road to a Jewish State, it must be mercilessly sacrificed in favour of the one ideal. One should remember that one may have many ideas and respect them highly, but one can have only one ideal. To this ideal all other ideals must bow, and near it there should not and cannot exist a "second" ideal, for two ideals are as absurd as two gods: one can worship only one G-d and only one ideal. Everything else one may like is, and must remain, of secondary importance."

Questions:

1. What do you think Jabotinsky meant by "modified Zionism?"
2. Why didn't the Jews of Europe and the U.S. heed Jabotinsky's call to mass immigration to Palestine in the 1920s and 30s? Would a numerical superiority have made a difference?
3. What did Jabotinsky intend by the phrase, "political offensive?" How effective is Israel's "political offensive" today? How can we help?
4. Explain the phrase, "the extent of responsibility depends on what is given?"
5. In the last paragraph of this essay, Jabotinsky states that the Jewish youth must devote themselves completely to the sole task of building up the Jewish state. Do you agree with this?"

Revisionist Zionism *page 2 of 2*

"Zionism springs from an even deeper motive

than Jewish suffering.

It is rooted in a Jewish spiritual tradition

whose maintenance and development

are for Jews the basis

of their continued existence

as a community."

(Albert Einstein)

The Pioneering Spirit

MISCONCEPTION: The indigenous Arab inhabitants lived in Palestine from time immemorial until the invading Zionist colonialists displaced them at the end of the 19th century.

REALITY: The Land of Israel was "monotonous and uninviting" (Mark Twain) – a barren, backward province of the Ottoman Empire with scarcely any native inhabitants. Ironically, it was the very success of the Zionist pioneers that attracted Arabs from the newly formed neighbouring countries into the land.

Objectives:

- Analyse the motivation of the young people who immigrated to the Land of Israel during the period of the Second *Aliyah* (1904–1914).
- Understand who they were and why they are called "*Chalutzim*."
- Examine the accomplishments of the *Chalutzim*.
- Realise how we can learn from their example.

A: Introduction and Motivation

1. Students will read in pairs Worksheet #1 ("Innocents Abroad") by Mark Twain describing the Land of Israel in the 19th century.
2. Suggestion: view a clip of Israel today from Jerusalem U's "Israel Inside, How a Small Nation Makes a Difference." (or a similar film)
3. Ask: "How did the land change so much in 100 years? (The answer: Through the work of people. Who were these people? The *Chalutzim*, who are the subject of this unit.)

TUVIA

B: The Chalutzim (Pioneers)

1. Ask the following questions:
   - How many of you would classify your socio-economic status as middle class?
   - How many of you would like to attend university?
   - Have you engaged in hard physical labour over an extended period of time in your life? (The answer to the first two questions will probably be yes and the third no).

2. Inquire, "What would cause you to leave your home and walk thousands of miles to a new one?" (Give the students time to formulate their answers).

3. Inform students that: "Many *Chalutzim* came from similar backgrounds and were close in age to you. What caused them to leave their homes, their parents, siblings and friends in order to settle in a 'hopeless dreary, heartbroken land'"? (Twain)

4. Write the students' answers on the board. On one side write positive reasons such as "the dream to return to and rebuild Zion." On the other side write negative factors such as "pogroms." Inform the students that we will now examine how these reasons play out in reality.

5. Students will read and complete Worksheet #2, ("The City of Slaughter") by Bialik. This work will initially be done in pairs and then discussed in a class format.

6. In order to help students understand what a *Chalutz/a* is, they should read and complete Worksheet #3, (Personal Statements of *Chalutzim*).

7. Write the slogan of the Second *Aliyah* on the board: אנו באנו ארצה לבנות ולהיבנות בה. ("We came to this Land to build it and be built up by it"). Explain the literal and figurative meaning of this statement. What three things did the *Chalutzim* want to "conquer?"
   a) Land
   b) Language
   c) Defense
   Elaborate on each answer.

8. Rachel: An example of a chalutza par excellence. Distribute Worksheet #4, Rachel Bluwstein's biography and two of her poems, "Maybe" and "To My Land." Review her biography with the students and discuss the poems. Suggestion: Play the music which accompanies the poems. Some ideas for discussion:
   - In the poem "Maybe" Rachel wistfully reflects on the perfection of her life at the kibbutz and thinks that since it was so ideal, maybe it was a dream.
   - In the poem/ode "To my Land" Rachel is asking herself and the reader what the purpose of our life is.
   - How can we be heroes? Must we "glorify G-d's name with deeds of heroism or with the spoils of war?" Or is it enough to "plant a tree on the quiet shores of the Jordan?"

C: Conclusion:

"As the plows begin to do their work, the Jews return to their history... As they take the physical labour of tiling the earth, they transform themselves from object to subject, from victims to sovereigns." *

– Ari Shavit

The previous discussion should lead to an awareness of the selflessness of the early *Chalutzim* who planted trees where none had grown for generations and cultivated the soil in order to recreate a beautiful land that many pioneers would never live to see. The fact that they toiled for the future Jewish people in a future homeland was truly a heroic endeavour. Conclude by attempting to define heroism using the *Chalutzim* as an example.

TUVIA

- Were the *Chalutzim* heroes? How do we define a hero? Have the students come up with a list of adjectives and attributes that they feel define heroism.
- Ask: "In what ways were the *Chalutzim* heroes?"
- How did these heroes contribute to the development of the State of Israel?
- We all have the potential to be selfless and make the world a better place.

*"We came to this land
to build it and to be built up by it"*

(Chalutzim)

"אנו באנו ארצה
לבנות ולהיבנות בה"

(חלוצים)

---

* Shavit, Ari, *My Promised Land, The Triumph and Tragedy of Israel*, (Spiegel & Grau: New York, 2013)

WORKSHEET #1

Name: _____   Date: _____

"The Innocents Abroad"
Mark Twain

DEPARTURE FROM JERUSALEM (CHAPTER 56)

TUVIA

"So ends the pilgrimage. We ought to be glad that we did not make it for the purpose of feasting our eyes upon fascinating aspects of nature, for we should have been disappointed – It truly is "monotonous and uninviting," and there is no sufficient reason for describing it as being otherwise.

Of all the lands there are for dismal scenery, I think Palestine must be the prince. The hills are barren, they are dull of color, they are unpicturesque in shape. The valleys are unsightly deserts fringed with a feeble vegetation that has an expression about it of being sorrowful and despondent. The Dead Sea and the Sea of Galilee sleep in the midst of a vast stretch of hill and plain wherein the eye rests upon no pleasant tint, no striking object, no soft picture dreaming in a purple haze or mottled with the shadows of the clouds. Every outline is harsh, every feature is distinct, there is no perspective – distance works no enchantment here. It is a hopeless, dreary, heart-broken land."

The Innocents Abroad was Mark Twain's second book and a great success. Within its first year it sold over 70,000 copies, and it remained his best-selling book throughout his lifetime. The book was published in 1869 and is based on Twain's visit to the Holy Land and surrounding countries in 1867.

Question:
How did the land change so much since Mark Twain's observation?

Name: _____   Date: _____

In the City of Slaughter
Chaim Nachman Bialik

CHAIM NACHMAN BIALIK (1873–1934) was born in the Ukrainian village of Radi (Radomyshl) and lived in Odessa for much of his adult life and then moved to Tel Aviv in 1924. Bialik is inevitably called the finest and most influential modern Hebrew poet. In his lifetime, he was hailed as the poet laureate of Jewish nationalism. His poetry epitomised the rise of Zionism and of Hebrew as a living language. A number of his folk poems have frequently been set to music. "In the City of Slaughter" was the poem that made Bialik famous when it appeared in 1903 as one of a series of "poems of wrath."

Kishinev, in Russia, has been seared into Jewish consciousness as the place in which one of the most publicised pogroms of its age took place. In 1903, forty-nine Jews were murdered and 500 were injured. Seven hundred houses were looted and destroyed, as were six hundred shops and businesses. This event prompted Chaim Nachman Bialik to write his famous poem, בעיר ההרגה ("In the City of Slaughter"), one of the classics of Hebrew literature. Below are excerpts from this epic poem:

> "Arise, go forth to the city of the slaughter, and come to the courtyards,
> And with your own eyes you will see, and with your hand you will feel on the fences,
> on the trees, on the stones, and on the plaster on the walls;
> The congealed blood, and the hardened brains of the corpses.
> Come from here to the ruins, and pass over the breaches,
> pass by the broken walls and smashed ovens;
> In the place where the destroyer's shattering deepened, widened, and enlarged the holes...
> For G-d called forth the spring and the slaughterer together:
> The sun shone, the Acacia blossomed, and the slaughterer slaughtered.
> You flee, and come to the courtyard; in the courtyard is a heap.
> On this heap, two are beheaded: A Jew and his dog.
> One axe beheaded them, and on to the rubbish heap they were thrown...
> They lay in their shame and they saw; they didn't move or budge;
> They didn't gouge out their eyes; they didn't go out of their minds.
> Perhaps a man even prayed, to himself, in his heart.
> "Ribono Shel Olam! Perform a miracle! May this evil not come come upon me."
> Those that defiled the defilement, and arose from the blood –
> Behold their lives became abhorrent, the light of their world was defiled,
> An eternal abomination, an impurity of body and soul – outside and inside.

continued on next page

50

Their husbands dashed forth from their holes and ran to the House of G-d.

They blessed G-d for the miracle of their salvation and deliverance.

The Kohanim amongst them went to ask their rabbis:

"Rabbi – my wife…. Is she, now, permitted or forbidden for me?"

And all will return to normal. All will go back to the way it was.

Now go, and I will bring you to all the hiding places: Outhouses, pig-pens, and other filthy places.

You will see with your eyes where they were hiding,

Your brothers, the sons of your people, descendents of the Macabees,

Offspring of the "lions" of the "Av HaRachamim," the seed of the "Kedoshim";

Twenty people to a hole, thirty more here and thirty there.

They magnified My glory in the world, and sanctified My name among the masses.

Like scampering mice they fled, they hid like fleas

And died the death of dogs, there where they were found…

You'll cry out for the kindness of the nations, and pray for the pity of the Goyim.

Just as you've been schnorrers before, you'll be schnorrers again.

Now, why are you here, son of man? Arise flee to the desert.

Carry with you there the cup of sorrow.

Rip apart your soul there into ten pieces.

Give your heart as food to a rage that is without force…"

Chaim Nachman Bialik (5664/1903)

Questions:

1. What do you think Bialik was trying to convey with the following line: "The sun shone, the Acacia blossomed, and the slaughterer slaughtered?"
2. Who is Bialik criticizing in his poem?
3. What advice is he offering in the last stanza?
4. What did you think of the excerpts of the poem that you read?

In the City of Slaughter *page 2 of 2*

WORKSHEET #3

Name: _____ Date: _____

Personal Statements of *Chalutzim*

TUVIA

RACHEL BLUWSTEIN (1890–1931) was born in Russia and arrived in Israel at the age of nineteen. She first worked as a labourer in Rehovot and later joined a training farm near the Kinneret. In 1913 Rachel left the Land of Israel for France in order to study agriculture. Unable to return to the Ottoman province of Palestine during the War, she traveled to Russia to work at an orphanage, where she contracted tuberculosis. In 1919 she returned to the Land of Israel and for a while lived in Deganya until her illness forced her to spend the last years of her life in Jerusalem and Tel Aviv. She fell in love with the landscapes and personalities in the Galilee. Rachel considered herself destined to collect the echoes and memories preserved in the vestiges of abandoned sites around the Kinneret. In a note entitled "On the Shores of Kinneret," she wrote the following:

THE SITE OF A DESTINY

"We rise at dawn with the feeling that if we were to wake up just one minute earlier we would surprise the night and penetrate the mystery of its murmur. We first looked at the lake, still plunged in sleep at that hour, entirely black and framed by still slumbering blue mountains.

Dawn had not entirely broken before we began working. We were fourteen in all, barefoot and with callused hands, completely tanned, scratched everywhere and with hardened faces and ardent hearts. The air was filled with our songs and debates and laughter. The movement of shovels never stopped as we paused for only brief moments to wipe the sweat pouring down our foreheads with our kefia, the time to look quickly and lovingly at the lake. How blue it was. Blue, blue, blue. Not a word. A message of peace, a remedy for the soul. A veil floated over the water.

Once again in the fields, towards midday, we returned to the lake like to a blue eye gazing upon us through the dining hall window. The blue eye of this corner of our country. Our voices were all the gayer for the modesty of the meal. Far from all satiety, destined to be martyred, to the torments and the chains, yet resolved nonetheless to sanctify the name of our country.

---

continued on next page

I remember having planted a eucalyptus, with the others, in the middle of the swamps where the Jordan leaves the lake and flows quickly towards the desert, spraying against the rocks, overrunning its banks.

On occasion, one of us shivered with fever on her poor mattress but none of us ever lost, even momentarily, this feeling of gratitude that we had for our destiny, for we worked ardently and enthusiastically.

When we were thirsty, one of us would go get water in a utensil, generally a can that had contained gasoline. What pleasure to run along the rocky shore and drink deeply like wild beasts! To plunge our burning faces into the water, raise them to the wind and drink once again until we were exhausted. It is said that these waters possess miraculous powers; that whoever drinks of them, even once, is drawn back. Thus we might imagine that it is because our ancestors satisfied their thirst at this lake that Jews in the Diaspora feel so much nostalgia for its peaceful beaches.

On Saturdays I usually took walks, resting gladly on the heights surrounding us. There were hidden corners, shaded spots and green valleys. Oh to spend your entire life here, walking along the shore, until you reach the walls surrounded by round towers, of Tiberias! This very ancient city seemed no more real to me than a sketch in an old sketchpad. Lake Kinneret is no ordinary landscape or even a corner of nature. It is the site of a people's destiny. Here, our past winks its thousand eyes and rocks us in its thousand lips. Rachel, On the Shores of Lake Kinneret."

TUVIA

JOSEPH TRUMPELDOR (1880–1920) was born in Russia. He joined the Russian army in 1902 and served in the Russian-Japanese War two years later. During the siege of Port Arthur he lost his left arm and was taken prisoner, receiving a high Tsarist order of merit for his gallantry and zeal. In 1912 he settled in Israel and for a while lived at Deganya. He was a founder of the *Zion Mule Corps* in 1915 and saw action in Gallipoli where he was shot through the shoulder. At the end of the war, Trumpeldor returned to Russia where he witnessed the Russian Revolution. In 1918 he established *He-Halutz*, the pioneering youth organisation that prepared youngsters for settlement in Israel.

Following his return to Israel and his involvement in the defense of Tel Hai, a settlement in the Galilee, against the Arabs, he was fatally wounded. He was killed together with seven other defenders and it is claimed that as he lay on his deathbed, one of his final utterances was, "Never mind, it is good to die for one's country."

Personal Statements of *Chalutzim* *page 2 of 3*

WORKSHEET #3

"I AM THAT WHEEL"

"We must establish a generation of Jews without interests or habits. They must simply be like a bar of steel. Malleable but malleable like steel, the type of metal that can be forged into whatever is necessary for the nation's furnace. "Is a wheel missing? I'm that wheel! Perhaps there's no screw or piston? Take me! Is someone needed to dig up the earth? I'm a digger! Is a soldier needed? I'm a soldier! What else is needed a policeman, a doctor, a lawyer, a teacher, a fetcher of water? Please turn to me; I can do all of these things. I have no face, no psychology, no emotions, nothing whatsoever. What am I? I'm the pure idea of service, ready at all times, unburdened by any prior commitment. I respond to only one command: Go out and build!"

(Formulated by Joseph Trumpeldor in a conversation with Ze'ev Jabotinsky in 1916)

Question:
What do Rachel Bluwstein's and Joseph Trumpeldor's statements tell you about the mind-set of the *Chalutzim*?

Personal Statements of *Chalutzim* *page 3 of 3*

WORKSHEET #4

Name: _____ Date: _____

Poetry of Rachel Bluwstein (1890–1931)

TUVIA

Rachel's poetry is set in the pastoral countryside of Israel, although her personal struggles add a sad and nostalgic mood to their reading. Many of her poems were set to music both during her lifetime and thereafter. She is buried in the Kibbutz Kinneret cemetery alongside many of the socialist ideologues and pioneers of the second and third waves of immigration (*Aliyot*) to Israel.

<table>
<tr><td>

Perhaps

Perhaps all this never was,
Perhaps I never rose at dawn to till
The garden by the sweat of my brow?

Nor even on long burning harvest days
Atop a sheaf-laden cart
Raised my voice in song?

Never purified myself in the quiet blue and innocence
Of my Kinneret,

Oh Kinneret,
did you truly exist?
Or were you only a dream?

1927

</td><td>

ואולי

ואולי לא היו הדברים מעולם
ואולי מעולם,
לא השכמתי עם שחר לגן
לעבדו בזיעת אפי?

מעולם, בימים ארוכים
בימים ארוכים ויוקדים של קציר
במרומי עגלה עמוסת אלומות
לא נתתי קולי בשיר?

מעולם לא טהרתי בתכלת שוקטה ובתום
של כנרת שלי

הו כנרת שלי
ההיית, או חלמתי חלום?

תרפ"ז

</td></tr>
</table>

continued on next page

To My Land

I have not sung your praises, my land,
Or celebrated your heroic deeds
With the spoils of war
Only one tree I planted on the way
Which to the Jordan leads
Only one narrow path to my feet yields
Which runs across the fields.

I know how humble are the gifts
The child offers her mother:
A cry of joy one glorious day,
When shines the sun in splendour,
And, shed for you, a secret tear,
To see the shabby clothes you wear.

Tel Aviv 1926

אל ארצי

לא שרתי לך ארצי,
ולא פארתי שמך
בעלילות גבורה,
בשלל קרבות:
רק עץ – ידי נטעו
חופי ירדן שוקטים,
רק שביל – כבשו רגלי
על פני שדות:

אכן דלה מאוד–
ידעתי זאת, האם,
אכן דלה מאוד
מנחת בתך:
רק קול תרועת הגיל
ביום יגה האור,
רק בכי במסתרים
עלי עניך:

תל־אביב, תרפ"ו

Kinneret

There, the heights of the Golan, you would caress them
By stretching out a hand,
Suggest a serene and silent pause,
There, the venerable Hermon,
In its radiant solitude,
The immaculate crown
Sends me its wind.

There, on the lake shore, a small palm tree
With its tousled branches
Like a mischievous child
Running along the lake shore to dip his feet
Into the waters of Kinneret…

Tel Aviv, 1927

כנרת

שם הרי גולן, הושט היד וגע בם
בדממה בוטחת מצווים: עצור!
בבדידות קורנת נם חרמון הסבא
וצינה נושבת מפסגת הצחור.

שם על חוף הים יש דקל שפל צמרת,
סתור שיער הדקל כתינוק שובב:
שגלש למטה ובמי כנרת
משכשך רגליו...

תל־אביב, תרפ"ז

Questions:

1. What is Rachel pondering in her "Perhaps" poem?
2. What is Rachel asking the reader in her ode "To My Land"?
3. What was your reaction to her poetry (language, imagery and tone)?

The British Mandate (1917–1948)

Part One: The Hope

MISCONCEPTION: The benevolent British Mandate, based on the Balfour Declaration, was good for the Jews.

REALITY: The British reneged on their favourable promises to the Jews within a very short space of time and their policies during their Mandate fanned the flames of conflict that dominate the Middle East today.

The British Mandate, Part One

Objectives:

- Examine the British Mandate of Palestine (1917–1948).
- Understand how the Jews in the Land of Israel helped bring the British into Israel and finally were a factor in their ignominious departure.
- Analyse how the policies of Great Britain are the root cause of many of the problems in the Middle East today.

A: Introduction and Motivation

1. Students read in pairs Worksheet #1 ("The Balfour Declaration") and attempt to answer the questions.
2. Examine Worksheet #3, (Maps of Ottoman Empire Before and After WWI) Note: The idea in this introduction is to generate discussion, not to necessarily reach definitive conclusions. These will be arrived at during the course of this unit.

TUVIA

B: The British Mandate

1. Review the details of WWI:
   a) What were the **MAIN** reasons for the outbreak?
      - **M**illitarism
      - **A**lliances
      - **I**ndustrialization
      - **N**ationalism
   b) Who was fighting whom? (Great Britain, France, Russia, and Italy vs. Germany, Austria-Hungary and the Ottoman Empire)

2. Explain how initially, the neutral American/ Zionist Jewish sympathies were with the German side (because of the shared hatred of Tsarist Russia). However, as the war continued, the hope grew for an Allied victory in order to oust the Ottoman Empire from the Land of Israel.

3. In order to aid the Allied forces, the Jews from the Land of Israel utilised three means:
   a) The Zion Mule Corps (1915)
   b) The Jewish Legion (1917) and
   c) Nili (1915–1917).

   Elucidate each one, with the aid of Worksheet #4 if necessary.

4. Discuss the Balfour Declaration (Worksheet #1) and the post-war peace conferences. The British issued the Balfour Declaration for a few different reasons:
   - To justify their presence in the Middle East (specifically on the other side of the Suez Canal). After the war the British were to be the custodians of a future Jewish State. (The Balfour Declaration was included in the preamble of the League of Nations Mandate for Palestine).
   - The Zionist sympathies of some members of the British Cabinet (Balfour, Samuel, Lloyd-George). These people also felt that Great Britain was indebted to the famous scientist and Zionist leader Chaim Weitzman, who had found a way to synthetically produce acetone (a key component for munitions desperately needed by the British at the front). Additionally, they felt that the Declaration would express their gratitude to the Jews for their contribution in the Allied war effort.
   - The British cabinet had an exaggerated sense of the "Jewish influence" in other countries. They felt that a pro-Jewish Declaration would force the U.S. into the war as well as keep Russia in the war.

5. Review Worksheet # 2, The McMahon Letter, and discuss. A month after the issue of the Balfour declaration, the British entered Jerusalem (December 17th) on the first day of Chanukah. Jewish joy knew no bounds. There was great hope that a Jewish home in the Land of Israel was now within sight. Suggestion: Show clip from "Pillar of Fire (volume 2)."

6. Re-examine Worksheet #3 and see how Great Britain and France had divided up the Middle East and created a new reality. They had created states where none had existed before. Discuss this phenomenon and its potential implications.

7. Britain's first High Commissioner of Palestine was Sir Herbert Samuel, a Jew and a Zionist. In fact, on his first *Shabbat* in Jerusalem he attended services at the Churva Synagogue and was given the honour of maftir. The *Shabbat* was "Nachamu," the *Shabbat* of comfort after Tisha b'Av. The Jews in attendance were moved to great emotion. For the first time in almost two thousand years, a Jew was governing the Jewish Homeland.

C: Conclusion:

After an extremely auspicious beginning, the remaining years of the Mandate were marked by Britain's betrayal of the Jews and their reneging on the Balfour Declaration. This radical change of policy will be examined in the following unit.

TUVIA

"Comfort my people, comfort them says your G-d. Speak to the heart, Jerusalem..."

(Isaiah 40:1–2)

"נַחֲמוּ נַחֲמוּ עַמִּי יֹאמַר אֱלֹהֵיכֶם:
דַּבְּרוּ עַל-לֵב יְרוּשָׁלַ‍ִם..."

(ישעיה מ:א-ב)

Name:_____ Date:_____

The Balfour Declaration (November 2, 1917)

During the First World War British policy gradually became committed to the idea of establishing a Jewish home in Palestine (*Eretz Yisrael*). After discussions in the British Cabinet and consultation with Zionist leaders, the decision was made known in the form of a letter by Lord Arthur James Balfour to Lord Rothschild. The letter represents the first political recognition of Zionist aims by a Great Power.

> Foreign Office
> November 2nd, 1917
>
> Dear Lord Rothschild,
>
> I have much pleasure in conveying to you, on behalf of His Majesty's Government, the following declaration of sympathy with Jewish Zionist aspirations which has been submitted to, and approved by, the Cabinet.
>
> "His Majesty's Government view with favour the establishment in Palestine of a national home for the Jewish people, and will use their best endeavours to facilitate the achievement of this object, it being clearly understood that nothing shall be done which may prejudice the civil and religious rights of existing non-Jewish communities in Palestine, or the rights and political status enjoyed by Jews in any other country."
>
> I should be grateful if you would bring this declaration to the knowledge of the Zionist Federation.
>
> Yours sincerely,
> *Arthur James Balfour*

Balfour Draft (August 1917)

"His Majesty's Government accepts the principle that Palestine should be reconstituted as the national home of the Jewish people and will use its best endeavours to secure the achievement of this object and will be ready to consider any suggestions on the subject which the Zionist Organisation may desire to lay before it."

Questions:
1. What differences are there between the initial draft and the final declaration?
2. What is the significance of the altered document?
3. Why do you think Great Britain would issue such a declaration?

WORKSHEET #2

Name:_____ Date: _____

The McMahon Letter (October 24th, 1915)

The Arab propaganda machine uses the "McMahon Letter" to explain and prove that the British had promised them the Land of Israel before it was promised to the Jews in the Balfour Declaration. However, a close reading of the text proves that this isn't so. The territory excluded from the agreement (typed in bold) was in fact where the future State of Israel would be established. Palestine was not a "twice promised land."

October 24, 1915

Dear Husain Ali, Sherif of Mecca:

I have received your letter of the 29th Shawal, 1333, with much pleasure and your expressions of friendliness and sincerity have given me the greatest satisfaction.

I regret that you should have received from my last letter the impression that I regarded the question of the limits and boundaries with coldness and hesitation; such was not the case, but it appeared to me that the time had not yet come when that question could be discussed in a conclusive manner.

I have realised, however, from your last letter that you regard this question as one of vital and urgent importance. I have, therefore, lost no time in informing the Government of Great Britain of the contents of your letter, and it is with great pleasure that I communicate to you on their behalf the following statement, which I am confident you will receive with satisfaction: –

The two districts of Mersina and Alexandretta and portions of Syria lying to the west of the districts of Damascus, Homs, Hama and Aleppo cannot be said to be purely Arab, and should be excluded from the limits demanded. With the above modification,and without prejudice of our existing treaties with Arab chiefs, we accept those limits.

As for those regions lying within those frontiers wherein Great Britain is free to act without detriment to the interest of her ally, France, I am empowered in the name of the Goverment of Great Britain to give the following assurances and make the following reply to your letter...

Subject to the above modifications, Great Britain is prepared to recognise and support the independence of the Arabs in all the regions within the limits demanded by the Sherif of Mecca.

I am convinced that this declaration will assure you beyond all possible doubt of the sympathy of Great Britain towards the aspirations of her friends the Arabs and will result in a firm and lasting alliance, the immediate results of which will be the expulsion of the Turks from the Arab countries and the freeing of the Arab peoples from the Turkish yoke, which for so many years has pressed heavily upon them...

Henry McMahon
British High Commissioner, Cairo

WORKSHEET #3

Name:_____ Date:_____

Maps of The Ottoman Empire
Before and After World War One

Ottoman Empire Before WWI:

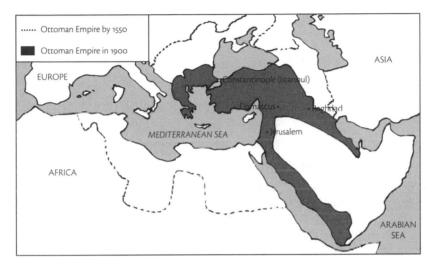

British Mandate of Palestine after WWI (1922):

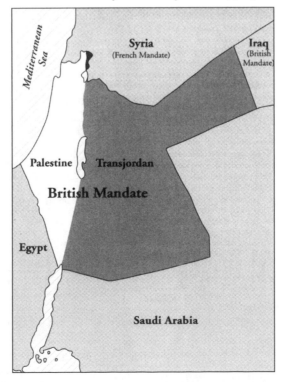

WORKSHEET #4

Name:_____ Date:_____

The Zionist Contribution to Great Britain's War Effort

ZION MULE CORPS 1915

The idea of a Jewish fighting unit in the British armed forces was first raised on December 1914 by Vladimir Jabotinsky. This was supported by Yosef Trumpeldor, a Zionist who had been the first Jewish military officer in the Russian Army, an honour earned by outstanding bravery. By the end of March 1915, 500 Jewish volunteers from among the Jews in Egypt (deported by the Turks) had started training. The British military command initially opposed the participation of Jewish volunteers on the Palestinian front or in an infantry unit and suggested that the volunteers serve instead as a detachment for mule transport on some other sector of the Turkish front. Trumpeldor succeeded in forming the 650-strong Zion Mule Corps, of whom 562 were sent to the Gallipoli front where Trumpeldor led his troops with great distinction. The bravery and courage of the men in the Corps was a key factor in convincing the British to establish Jewish Infantry Brigades, known as the Jewish Legion.

> "The men have done extremely well, working their mules calmly under heavy shell and rifle fire, and thus showing a more difficult type of bravery than the men in the front line who had the excitement of combat to keep them going."
>
> (General Sir Ian Hamilton, British commander at Gallipoli to Jabotinsky)

JEWISH LEGION 1917

Jabotinsky pursued his project of a Jewish Legion for the Palestinian front. Finally, on August 1917, the formation of a Jewish regiment was officially announced. Jabotinsky was commissioned as an officer in the unit. The unit was designated as the 38th Battalion of the Royal Fusiliers and included British volunteers, members of the former Zion Mule Corps and a large number of Russian Jews. In April of 1918, the 39th Battalion of the Royal Fusiliers joined it, more than 50 percent of whom were American volunteers. The unit fought with distinction against the Ottoman Turks and was the first British force to cross the Jordan River. They were assigned a menorah with the Hebrew word "Kadima" (forward/east) as their unit insignia. This was the first Jewish fighting force fighting in the Land of Israel since Bar Kochba's insurrection against Rome in the second century of the Common Era.

continued on next page

NILI 1915–1917

Nili was a secret, pro-British spying organisation which operated under Turkish rule in Palestine during World War I under the leadership of the world-famous agronomist Aaron Aaronsohn, Sarah Aaronsohn, Yosef Lishansky and Avshalom Feinberg. The organisation's name was an acronym for the Hebrew verse "*Netzah Yisrael Lo Yeshaker* – the strength of Israel will not deceive" (1 Samuel 15:29), which served as its password.

Nili was founded by a number of Jews in the *moshavot* (settlements) who believed that the future of the Jews depended upon the Land of Israel (*Eretz Yisrael*) being taken over by Britain. The group did not enjoy the full support of all the Jews in the Land of Israel. In February 1917, contact was first established between the espionage center in Atlit and British intelligence in Cairo. The connections were maintained by sea for several months during which the British received invaluable information, including Turkish troop positions and water deposits collected by the group.

The Turks later uncovered the network and in October 1917, Turkish soldiers surrounded Zichron Ya'akov and arrested numerous people, including Aaronsohn's sister, Sarah, who committed suicide after four days of torture. Before she died she wrote a letter to Aaron in which she stated:

"I haven't the strength to suffer any more…in vain did they try all kinds of tortures on us. We did not speak…I aspired to save my people."

After the war, one British Officer stated, in acknowledging the debt of the British to Nili:

"It was very largely the daring work of young spies, most of them natives of Palestine, which enabled the brilliant Field Marshal (Allenby) to accomplish his undertaking so effectively. The leader (in Palestine) of the spy system was a young Jewess, a Miss Sarah Aaronsohn."

TUVIA

The Zionist Contribution to Great Britain's War Effort *page 2 of 2*

"As long as deep in the heart,

The soul of a Jew yearns

And towards the East

An eye looks to Zion.

Our hope is not yet lost,

The hope of two thousand years;

To be a free people in our land,

The land of Zion and Jerusalem."

(Naphtali Herz Imber, 1886)

The British Mandate (1917–1948)

Part Two:
The Betrayal

MISCONCEPTION: The Palestinian Arabs have never been offered a State of their own.

REALITY: The Mandate of Palestine was already partitioned into an Arab and Arab/Jewish entity by the Churchill White Paper of 1922. The Arabs of Palestine subsequently rejected two further partition offers that would have resulted in another Arab state in the Middle East (The Peel Partition Plan of 1937, and the UN Partition Plan of 1947) in part, because these plans would also have created a Jewish State which was unacceptable to them. In 2000 Israel offered the Palestian Authority a two-state solution that was summarily rejected for the same reason.

Objectives:

- Examine the British Mandate of Palestine (1917–1948).
- Understand how the Jews in the Land of Israel helped bring the British into Israel and finally were a factor in their inglorious departure.
- Study the "Tower and Stockade" and "*Aliyah Bet*" responses of the *Yishuv*.
- Analyse how the policies of Great Britain are the root cause of many of the problems in the Middle East today.

A: Introduction and Motivation

1. Read through Worksheet #1, Preamble and Article 5 of the League of Nations Mandate for Palestine. Note that honouring the Balfour Declaration was an integral part of the Mandate agreement. In addition, the British agreed not to change any of the borders of the Mandate (article 5).

2. Suggestion: show clips from "The Long Way Home" of the *Aliyah Bet* ship "Exodus 1947" and the explosion of the King David Hotel. Ask: " How do you think it is possible that the British, who were welcomed so enthusiastically by the Jews and the Zionist movement into the Land of Israel, became in a very short space of time so hated and were eventually driven out by the very same Jews?"

Arguably the British were the perpetrators of one of the greatest betrayals of the Jewish people and of Jewish hopes in the twentieth century.

TUVIA

B: British Betrayal

1. From almost the moment the British established their Mandate, they began negating their commitments to the Balfour declaration. The three main reasons for this were:
   - Now that Great Britain was in control of this strategic territory, they no longer needed the Jews.
   - In the early twenties, vast reserves of oil were discovered in Iraq and Saudi Arabia.
   - The British foreign office was filled with "Arabists" and Jew-haters.

2. The British appointment of Sir Herbert Samuel as the first High Commissioner of Palestine was a masterstroke. Because he was a Jew and a known Zionist, Samuel bent over backwards to show his neutrality and impartiality. It was during his tenure (1920–25) that the "Mandatory Cycle" that would characterise the British Mandate of Palestine began.

3. "Mandatory Cycle:" This consisted of four main components:

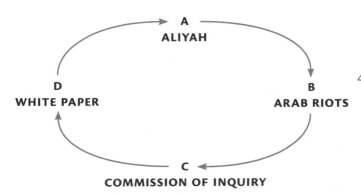

- **A) ALIYAH:** During the Mandate, there were three periods of mass Jewish immigration (*Aliyot*). These included: the Third *Aliyah* (1919–1923) which brought in 35,000 immigrants mainly from Poland and Russia; the Fourth *Aliyah* (1924–1928) which brought in 70,000 immigrants mainly from Poland; and the Fifth *Aliyah* (1929–1939) which brought in 235,000 from Europe, the majority fleeing Nazi persecution in Germany.
- **B) ARAB RIOTS:** The militant Arab response was to riot; after each *Aliyah* there were major riots (1920/1, 1929, 1936–9).
- **C) COMMISSIONS OF INQUIRY:** After each of the riots, the British Mandatory authorities established a commission of inquiry, ostensibly to investigate the cause of the rioting and determine how to prevent future outbreaks. In reality, the commissions placated the Arabs.
- **D) WHITE PAPERS:** These British statements of policy were issued at the conclusion of each commission (1922, 1930 and 1939). They were blatantly pro-Arab and aimed at appeasement. The Jewish response was, predictably, more immigration.

4. The White Papers indicated the direction of the British policy towards the Jews after the establishment of the Mandate. Let us now examine each one and answer the questions on Worksheet #2.

5. The Jewish response in the *Yishuv* was three-fold:
   I. ***Aliyah Bet*** ("Illegal Immigration" or "*HaApala*") – see Worksheet #4,
   II. ***Chomah U'Migdal*** ("Tower and Stockade) – see Worksheet #5, and
   III. **Armed defense and resistance** (*Haganah, Irgun, Lehi*) – see Worksheets #6 and #7.

6. Not all the soldiers of the British Mandate wholeheartedly supported the regime's increasingly anti-Jewish policies. One of the outstanding exceptions was Brigadier-General Charles Orde Wingate. Read Worksheet #8 and discuss the life of this Christian Zionist. He was a human being who acted on the strength of his convictions.

7. During WWII the young men and women of the *Yishuv* heeded Ben Gurion's call to "fight the White Paper as if there was no war, and to fight the war as if there was no White Paper." Whilst *Aliyah Bet* continued throughout the war (Worksheet #4) most Jewish men and women of fighting age in the Mandate volunteered for the British army or the Palmach. (This was in contrast with the Arabs of the Mandate who were largely pro-Nazi and whose leader, Haj Amein El-Husseini, spent the war in Berlin recruiting Muslims to the SS and sending hate-filled broadcasts on the radio). One of the most famous Jews of Mandatory Palestine who volunteered for the British army was Chana Szenesh. Read Worksheet #3 and answer the questions. Here is an example of a young woman (possibly with a similar background to the students) who made heroic selfless decisions in her life.

8. Despite having 100,000 servicemen in Palestine (to police 600,000 Jews), the British finally relinquished responsibility of the Mandate. This was largely a result of the United Jewish Resistance as well as world opinion. They handed over the "problem" to the UN who on November 29, 1947, voted to partition the Mandate into two states:
   - One for the Palestinian Jews (containing 80% desert)
   - One for the Palestinian Arab population (containing mostly arable land)

The Jews accepted this solution even though they were offered only 40% of the remaining 24% of the original Mandate, and Jerusalem (where 100,000 Jews lived) was to be an "international city." The Arabs rejected the whole partition plan and instigated what would become known as the War of Independence.

TUVIA

C: Conclusion:

Ask the students the following questions:

- If you had been alive during the British Mandate in Palestine, which underground movement would you have joined and why?
- Was *Aliyah Bet* effective? Why or why not?
- How are the British policies in the Middle East during the interwar period still a factor in the Middle East morass today?
- Suggested homework assignment: Read Elie Wiesel's "Dawn," a historical novella about the Jewish underground during the British Mandate. The story is based on an actual incident involving the *Irgun*. Answer the following question: "Do you agree with the actions of the protagonist, Elisha? Justify your answer."

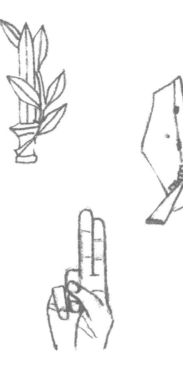

"The hope of 2000 years is to be
a free people in our land"

(Hatikvah)

"הַתִּקְוָה בַּת שְׁנוֹת אַלְפַּיִם
לִהְיוֹת עַם חוֹפְשִׁי בְּאַרְצֵנוּ"

(הַתִּקְוָה)

WORKSHEET #1

Name: _____   Date: _____

League of Nations Mandate for Palestine

PREAMBLE AND ARTICLE 5

"Preamble

The Council of the League of Nations:

WHEREAS the Principal Allied Powers have agreed, for the purpose of giving effect to the provisions of Article 22 of the Covenant of the League of Nations, to entrust to a Mandatory selected by the said Powers the administration of the territory of Palestine, which formerly belonged to the Turkish Empire, within such boundaries as may be fixed by them; and

WHEREAS the Principal Allied Powers have also agreed that the Mandatory should be responsible for putting into effect the declaration originally made on November 2nd, 1917, by the Government of His Britannic Majesty, and adopted the said Powers, in favour of the establishment in Palestine of a national home for the Jewish people, it being clearly understood that nothing should be done which might prejudice the civil and religious rights of existing non-Jewish communities in Palestine, or the rights and political status enjoyed by Jews in any other country; and

WHEREAS recognition has thereby been given to the historical connection of the Jewish people with Palestine and to the grounds for reconstituting their national home in that country; and

WHEREAS the Principal Allied Powers have selected the Britannic Majesty as the Mandatory for Palestine; and

WHEREAS the Mandate in respect of Palestine has been formulated in the following terms and submitted to the Council of the League for approval; and

WHEREAS His Britannic Majesty, has accepted the mandate in respect of Palestine and undertaken to exercise it on behalf of the League of Nations in conformity with the following provisions; and

WHEREAS by the afore-mentioned Article 22 (paragraph 8), it is provided that the degree of authority, control or administration to be exercised by the Mandatory, not having been previously agreed upon by the Members of the League, shall be explicitly defined by the Council of the League of Nations.

ARTICLE 5
The Mandatory shall be responsible for seeing that no Palestine territory shall be ceded to or leased to, or in any other way placed under the control of, the government of any foreign power."

Question:
Why did the British ignore their agreed obligations to the Jews?

WORKSHEET #2

Name: _____ Date: _____

The British Mandate White Papers

1922 — CHURCHILL WHITE PAPER:

Policy paper redefining British interpretation of the responsibilities to a Jewish National Home issued in 1922. The paper stated that the government did not wish to see Palestine become "as Jewish as England is English", but rather the establishment of "a center in which Jewish people as a whole may take, on grounds of religion and race, an interest and a pride." Jewish and Arab agencies were to be established to manage their own affairs.

The White Paper confirmed the right of Jewish immigration but stipulated that this should not exceed the "economic absorptive capacity" of the country. The east bank of the Jordan river – Transjordan – was no longer open for Jewish settlement. (In 1946 this territory achieved independence and was called The Hashemite Kingdom of Jordan.) This territory consisted of 76% of the area of the British Mandate of Palestine.

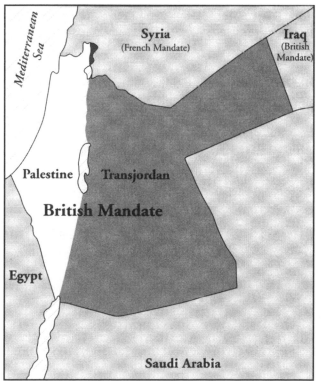

Most of the mandated territory earmarked for the "Jewish National Home" was unilaterally severed in 1922 by Great Britain to create a new Arab entity – Transjordan (now the Hashemite Kingdom of Jordan)

continued on next page

1930 — PASSFIELD WHITE PAPER:

British policy statement issued on October 21, 1930, following the Arab riots in Palestine and the recommendations of the Shaw Commission and the Hope-Simpson report. On the critical question of immigration, the sentiments of the paper were against a generous policy towards the Zionists. The Zionist movement mounted a major campaign against the White Paper and in a letter made public during February of 1931, British Prime Minister Ramsay MacDonald promised Chaim Weizmann what amounted to its abrogation.

1939 — MACDONALD WHITE PAPER:

Statement of British Palestine policy issued on May 17, 1939. Following the recommendation of the Woodhead Commission that partition was impracticable, a new policy for Palestine was issued. (This was after the Arabs rejected receiving 75% of Western Palestine offered by the Peel Partition Plan of 1937.)

Known as the MacDonald White Paper, it proposed the creation, within ten years, of a unitary Palestine state, with its borders from the Mediterranean to the Jordan River. The Paper also outlined a Five Year Plan for the immigration of seventy-five thousand Jews (ten thousand per annum and a further twenty-five thousand refugees) – but thereafter no further immigration without Arab consent. In a land-transfer regulations policy paper of March 1940, the British went on to severely restrict land sales.

The Zionist movement saw the White Paper as "an act of betrayal," believing that it would condemn the Jewish population to a minority status in the country as well as end any hopes of creating a Jewish State.

The publication of the White Paper should be understood within the wider context of the escalation of general hostilities prior to the outbreak of the Second World War. It should be viewed as being made irrespective of the dire straits of European Jewry under or threatened by Nazi rule. Under these circumstances, it was clear to foreign policy experts that it would not be in Britain's interests to offend the sensibilities of the Arab and Muslim world. The White Paper remained British policy until 1948 and only ended with the termination of the Mandate on May 14, 1948.

Questions:
1. Do you think the British justified their restrictions on Jewish immigration and land purchase?
2. What was the result of the MacDonald White Paper for the Jews trapped in Europe?
3. What do you think David Ben Gurion meant when he declared in 1939, "We will fight the White Paper as if there is no War and we will fight the War as if there is no White Paper?"

The British Mandate White Papers *page 2 of 2*

Name:_____   Date:_____

Chana Szenesh

CHANA SZENESH (1921–1944) through her brief but noteworthy life, became a symbol of idealism and self-sacrifice. Her poems, made famous in part because of her murder by Nazi supporters, reveal a woman imbued with hope, even in the face of adverse circumstances.

Szenesh, the daughter of an author and journalist, was born in Budapest, Hungary. She demonstrated her own literary talent from an early age, and she kept a diary from age 13 until shortly before her death. Although her family was assimilated, anti-Semitic sentiment in Budapest led her to involvement in Zionist activities, and she left Hungary for Palestine in 1939. She studied first at an agricultural school, and then settled at Kibbutz Sdot Yam. While there she wrote poetry, as well as a play about kibbutz life.

In 1943 Szenesh joined the British Army and volunteered to be parachuted into Europe with other Palestinian Jewish volunteers. The purpose of this operation was to help the Allied efforts in Europe and establish contact with partisan resistance fighters in an attempt to aid beleaguered Jewish communities. Szenesh trained in Egypt and was one of the thirty-three chosen to parachute behind enemy lines. With the goal of reaching her native Budapest, Szenesh was parachuted in March 1944 into Yugoslavia, and spent three months with Tito's partisans. Her idealism and commitment to her cause are memorialised in her poem "Blessed is the Match," which she wrote at this time.

On June 7, 1944, at the height of the deportation of Hungarian Jews, Szenesh crossed the border into Hungary. She was caught almost immediately by the Hungarian police, and although tortured cruelly and repeatedly over the next several months, refused to divulge any information. Even the knowledge that her mother was at risk and that she too might be harmed did not move Szenesh to cooperate with the police. At her trial in October of that year, Szenesh staunchly defended her activities and she refused to request clemency. Throughout her ordeal she remained steadfast in her courage, and when she was executed by a firing squad on November 7, she refused the blindfold, staring squarely at her executors and her fate.

In 1950, Szenesh's remains were brought to Israel and re-interred in the military cemetery on Mount Herzl. Her diary and literary works were later published, and many of her more popular poems, including "Walking to Caesarea" and "Blessed is the Match," have been set to music.

continued on next page

Seventeen-year-old Chana wrote the following in her diary. Less than a year after this entry she arrived on the shores of Israel.

> "I don't know whether I've mentioned that I've become a Zionist. This word stands for a tremendous number of things. To me it means, in short, that I now consciously and strongly feel a Jew, and am proud of it…One needs something to believe in, something for which one has a whole-hearted enthusiasm. One needs to feel that one's life has meaning, that one is needed in this world. Zionism fulfills this for me."
>
> (October 27, 1938)

Walking to Caesarea (1943)

Oh L-rd, My G-d

I pray that these things never end

The sand and the sea,

The rush of the waters,

The crash of the heavens,

The prayer of man.

הליכה לקיסריה

א-לי א-לי, שלא יגמר לעולם

החול והים.

רשרוש של המים,

ברק השמים,

תפילת האדם.

Below is the poem "Blessed is the Match" by Chana Szenesh written in Yugoslavia in 1944 on a mission with Jews from Israel to save fellow Jews during the Holocaust. This poem was written five years after Chana's *Aliyah* (move to Israel) as she reflected on her role as a Jewess while her people were being murdered in Europe. It is read all over Israel on *Yom Hazikaron*, (Memorial Day).

Blessed is the Match (1944)

Blessed is the match consumed in kindling flame.

Blessed is the flame that burns in
    the secret fastness of the heart.

Blessed is the heart with the strength to stop beating
    for honour's sake.

Blessed is the match consumed in the kindling flame.

אשרי הגפרור

אשרי הגפרור והצית לבבות.

אשרי הלהבה שבערה בסתרי לבבות.

אשרי הלבבות שידעו לחדול
בכבוד…

אשרי הגפרור והצית לבבות.

Questions:

1. What is the "match" in the poem? Why is it "blessed?"
2. What does Chana's poem reflect regarding the Jewish View of "Sanctity of Life?" When is it worth fighting for something?
3. How can we help Israel now in these trying times?
4. Chana was a heroine. Are people born heroes? What characteristics do heroes posses?

Chana Szenesh *page 2 of 2*

Name: _____   Date: _____

'Aliyah Bet/Ha'apala' (Clandestine Immigration)

Organised *Ha'apala* commenced in 1934 and ended in 1948 with the establishment of the State of Israel. It is one of the links in a long chain of tales of courage about Jews who risked their lives in order to immigrate and to help others immigrate to the Land of Israel (*Eretz Yisrael*) in a struggle to assert their rights to enter freely into the country.

The *Ha'apala* was part of a great struggle in an effort to create a Jewish majority in Palestine, to achieve recognition of the national rights of the Jews to their Land, and to open the gates to every Jew towards establishing a Jewish State in the Land of Israel.

During the fourteen ensuing years, the *Ha'apala* was responsible for bringing over 122,000 people to Palestine by land, sea and air. This number includes deportees to Mauritius, Hamburg and Cyprus. The 122,000 immigrants can be divided into three prominent periods of *Ha'apala*:

1934–39	Until the outbreak of World War II	21,530 people
1940–44	The War Years	16,456 people
1945–48	Until the establishment of the State of Israel	84,333 people

The clandestine immigrants – *Ma'apilim* – arrived from two main directions: from Europe, which after 1934 was beginning to feel the shadow of Nazism, and from the Eastern countries – Lebanon, Syria, Iraq, Persia, also Egypt and the North African countries.

THE *HA'APALA* AFTER WORLD WAR II

From the end of the War and up to the establishment of the State of Israel, the foremost and almost only means of immigration to Eretz Israel was carried out clandestinely. The progress of the *Ha'apala* became more efficient from year to year in pursuit of the main purpose, the opening of the gates of the Land of Israel to all Jews. The *Ha'apala* became a vast and complex organisation. It was firmly supported by the *Yishuv* – The Jewish population in Palestine – and world Zionism. Financial support was extended from the entire Jewish Diaspora, the foremost being American Jewry. Many countries, especially in Europe, were sympathetic to the cause and there existed the support of world public opinion for the struggle of the refugees and the means used for their rescue. The organised network of the *"Mossad l'Aliyah"* spread throughout Europe and its emissaries reached North Africa, the adjacent Islamic countries and also the U.S.A.

continued on next page

WORKSHEET #4

Against the organisation for the *Ha'apala* stood the British Government with its military force and intelligence department. Between the two warring parties ensued a bitter and fierce struggle for the rights of entry into the Land of Israel. By and large, the retaliation against the British aimed at damaging arms and equipment used in deterring the *Ha'apala*. Radar, patrol boats, and deportation ships were hit and damaged time and again. During this short but stormy period about 84,000 *Ma'apilim* arrived by sea, land, and various other routes.

The deportation of the *Ma'apilim* from Palestine was one of the means utilised by the British in their aim to discourage would-be immigrants.

After WWII, the British renewed the deportation of immigrants. About 42,000 were sent to the detention camps in Cyprus beginning in August 1946. The last of the deportees in Cyprus were finally liberated in February 1949. The British deliberately kept men of fighting age in Cyprus until the end of the War of Independence.

TUVIA

YETSIAT EUROPA TESHAZ – EXODUS 1947

Towards the end of the Mandate, the British decided to break the *Ha'apala* by forcibly returning the immigrants to Europe. The first ship against which the British decided to use their new strategy was the 'Exodus 1947'. After a struggle with six destroyers of the British Navy, the *Exodus* was captured mid-ocean, in international waters. Three Jews were killed, including an American volunteer crewman, Bill Bernstein, and many sustained injuries during the forcible boarding by the British. The vessel's 4,530 passengers were deported in three British transport ships to Hamburg, Germany.

The *Exodus* incident helped turn the tide of world opinion against the British and their inhumane policy. The sight of weakened Holocaust survivors being dragged by force onto prison ships and being taken back to Germany, against their will, by armed British troops witnessed by the entire world, including the UNSCOP committee, was what forced the world to realize the urgent need for a Jewish State. Murray Greenfield, one of the Haganah American volunteer crewmen recalled: "More than any other event of *Aliya Bet*, the *Exodus* captured the attention of the outside world. This was not only due to the plight of the Jews, but to the way the British mishandled the situation from the standpoint of public relations." *

* Joseph M Hochstein and Murray S. Greenfield, *The Jews Secret Fleet, The Untold Story of the North American Volunteers who Smashed the British Blockade*, (Gefen: Jerusalem/New York, 1999/5759)

'Aliyah Bet/Ha'apala' (Clandestine Immigration) *page 2 of 3*

THE STRUGGLE

The unarmed *Ma'apilim* struggled against the British destroyers and soldiers, who used water-jets and tear-gas in order to overpower the immigrants aboard the ships. Nevertheless, the *Ma'apilim* were not bereft of hope. The opposition to the British Army was, to the *Ma'apilim*, an expression of self-defense and a source of pride and power.

CONCLUSION

In summing up, it is important today to understand what the *Ha'apala* contributed to the establishment of the State of Israel:

The concentration of Jewish refugees in captured areas of Italy and Germany and the continuous pressure of the struggle of the Ha'apala *raised the issue to the international negotiating table with a force that made evasion impossible.*

THE UNIFICATION OF THE *YISHUV*

The action of the *Ha'apala* was one of the factors that united the various factions of the population irrespective of opinion or political party. This unifying focus on a common objective was essential in the struggle to establish the State.

Questions:
1. In your opinion, what made *Aliyah Bet* so effective?
2. Why do you think some young American Jews volunteered for the *Aliya Bet* organization?

'Aliyah Bet/Ha'apala' (Clandestine Immigration) *page 3 of 3*

WORKSHEET #5

Name:_____ Date:_____

Chomah U'Migdal (Tower and Stockade)

The *Chomah U'Migdal* (Tower and Stockade) settlements derived their name from the need to set up ready-made, overnight settlements to forestall Arab attack and British opposition. These settlements were first established in the mid- to late-1930s as a reaction to the widespread Arab riots.

The *Keren Kayemet LeYisrael* (Jewish National Fund) had acquired a large amount of land. In order to settle this land in the face of Arab hostility and British opposition, the settlements had to be established by surprise, even overnight, in order to insure their existence would be a *fait accompli* before any reaction could occur. Large parties of settlers and workers would leave for the new point at dawn in order to finish erecting the settlement by nightfall. The name *Chomah U'Migdal* was derived from the fact that the central elements of these pre-planned communities were the watchtower in the center and the stockade around the settlement. Some fifty such settlements were set up in the years 1936–39, which was prior to the publication of the restrictive 1939 White Paper that pushed immigration largely underground. The settlements, mostly in the Upper Galilee and the Beit Shean Valley, also preceded the outbreak of World War Two.

The prodigious settlement activity of the 1936–39 period continued over the next few years despite the official restrictions on *Aliyah*. The period leading up to the foundation of the State saw the creation of over ninety new settlements, many according to the same *Chomah U'Migdal* model of the earlier years. Throughout this period, special attention was paid to the idea of settling in certain strategic areas, considered vital for the existence of the future Jewish state. In this way, the idea developed that settlements were a strategic security asset that would both dictate future state borders and provide those borders with a major line of defense.

The settlements set up in the Negev in the early 1940s so impressed the members of UNSCOP (United Nations Special Committee On Palestine) visiting in 1947 that they decided that if the Jews could do so much in such a short space of time, then the Negev should become part of the Jewish State.

Question:
How did the *Chomah U'Migdal* projects affect the borders of the future Jewish State?

Name:_____ Date:_____

Jewish Resistance Groups
Under British Mandatory Rule 1918–1948

THE *HAGANAH*

The underground military organisation of the *Yishuv* operated in the Land of Israel from 1920 to 1948. The Arab riots in 1920 and 1921 reinforced the view that it was impossible to depend upon the British authorities and that the *Yishuv* needed to create an independent defense force completely free of foreign authority. In June 1920, the *Haganah* was founded.

During the first nine years of its existence, the *Haganah* was a loose organisation of local defense groups in the large towns and in several of the settlements. The Arab riots in 1921 brought about a complete change in the *Haganah's* status.

- The *Haganah* became a large network encompassing nearly all the youth and adults in the settlements, as well as several thousand members from each of the cities.
- The *Haganah* initiated a comprehensive training program for its members and organised officers' training courses.
- The *Haganah* established a central arms depot into which a continuous stream of light arms flowed from Europe.
- Simultaneously, the basis was laid for the underground production of arms.

The years of the Arab Revolt, 1936–1939, were the years in which the *Haganah* matured and developed from a militia into a military body. Although the British administration did not officially recognise the organisation, the British security forces cooperated with it by establishing a civilian militia. In the summer of 1938, Special Night Squads, or SNS, were established under the command of Captain Orde Wingate (Worksheet #8).

During the years of the riots, the *Haganah* protected the establishment of over fifty new settlements in new areas of the country. As a result of the British government's anti-Zionist policy, expressed in the White Paper of 1939, the *Haganah* supported "illegal immigration" and organised demonstrations against the British anti-Zionist policy.

With the outbreak of World War II, the *Haganah* faced new problems. It headed a movement of volunteers from which Jewish units were formed for service in the British army known as the Jewish Brigade. It also cooperated with British intelligence units and sent its personnel out on various commando missions in the Middle East. Another example of this cooperation was when it dropped thirty-two Jewish parachutists in 1943–44 behind enemy lines in the Balkans, in Hungary and in Slovakia (Worksheet #3, Chana Szenesh).

continued on next page

At the same time, the *Haganah* further established its independence during the war. A systematic program of training was instituted for the country's youth. In 1941 the *Haganah's* first mobilized regiment, the Palmach, came into being. At the end of the war, when it became clear that the British government had no intention of altering its anti-Zionist policy, the *Haganah* began an open, organised struggle against British Mandatory rule in the framework of a unified Jewish Resistance Movement, consisting of the *Haganah*, *Irgun Zevai Le'umi* (*Etzel*) and *Lohamei Herut Yisrael* (*Lehi*).

Haganah branches were established at Jewish DP (displaced person) camps in Europe while *Haganah* members accompanied the "illegal" immigrant boats. In the spring of 1947, David Ben Gurion took it upon himself to direct the general policy of the *Haganah*, especially in preparation for the impending Arab attack. On May 26, 1948, the Provisional Government of Israel decided to transform the *Haganah* into the regular army of the State, to be called "*Tz"va Haganah Le-Yisrael*" (*Tzahal*) The Israel Defense Forces. The *Haganah* at that time had approximately 30,000 members.

IRGUN TZEVAI LE'UMI (THE IRGUN) – "THE NATIONAL MILITARY ORGANISATION" (ABBREVIATION ETZEL, IZL)

This armed Jewish underground organisation was founded in 1931 by a group of *Haganah* commanders who left the *Haganah* in protest against its defense charter. The group split in April 1937 during the Arab riots. About half its members returned to the *Haganah*. The rest formed a new movement named, *Irgun Zevai Le'umi* (abbreviated *Etzel*), which was ideologically linked with the Revisionist Movement and accepted the authority of its leader, Vladimir Jabotinsky.

Etzel rejected the "restraint" (*Havlaga*) policy of the *Haganah* and carried out armed reprisals against Arabs, which were condemned by the Jewish Agency. The British authorities arrested many of its members; one of them, Shlomo Ben Yosef, was hanged for shooting at an Arab bus. After the publication of the White Paper in May 1939, *Etzel* directed its activities against the British Mandatory authorities.

At the outbreak of World War II the organisation declared a truce with Britain, which led to a second split (see *Lohamei Herut Yisrael*). *Etzel* members joined the British Army's Palestinian units and later the Jewish Brigade.

Beginning in 1943, Menahem Begin headed *Etzel*. In February 1944, *Etzel* declared war against the British administration. It attacked and blew up government offices, military installations, and police stations. *Etzel* joined the Jewish Resistance Movement and following its disintegration in August 1946 after bombing the King David Hotel, *Etzel* continued its attacks on British military and government objectives.

Jewish Resistance Groups *page 2 of 3*

WORKSHEET #6

In April 1947, four members of the organisation were hanged in Acre prison (Worksheet #7, Dov Gruner). In May of that year, *Etzel* broke into the fortress at Acre and freed forty-one prisoners. In July 1947, when three other *Etzel* members were executed, the IZL hanged two British sergeants.

After the Declaration of Independence, the *Etzel* high command offered to disband the organisation and integrate its members into the army of the new Jewish state. It was subsequently disbanded and full integration was achieved in September 1948, at which point *Etzel* had approximately 3,000 members.

LOHAMEI HERUT YISRAEL (ABBREVIATION *LEHI*)

This armed underground group was founded by Abraham "Yair" Stern in June 1940, after the *Irgun Zevai Le'umi* decided on a truce on armed activities against the British during the war. *Lehi* declared a continuation of the struggle against the British, opposed the voluntary enlistment of Jews into the British Army, and even attempted to contact representatives of the Axis.

During January and February 1942, clashes between members of the "Stern gang" and the British authorities reached their peak. The British forces reacted by arresting and killing leading members of the group. Abraham Stern himself was caught and killed by British police officers. In early 1944, *Lehi* resumed its operations, joining in the struggle against the British through affiliation with the Jewish Resistance Movement. During and after this period, *Lehi* carried out sabotage operations and armed attacks on British military objectives and government installations. In April 1947, *Lehi* began organising sabotage operations outside Palestine, mailing bombs to British statesmen.

In May 29, 1948, two weeks after the establishment of the State of Israel, members of *Lehi* joined the Israeli army. In Jerusalem, however, they continued to fight separately. After the assassination of the UN mediator, Count Folke Bernadotte, in Jerusalem in September 1948, an act that a group of *Lehi* members were suspected of carrying out, the Israeli authorities enforced the final disbanding of *Lehi* in Jerusalem. *Lehi* ceased to exist. *Lehi* had approximately 300 members when it disbanded.

Question:
Which underground movement would you have joined and why?

Jewish Resistance Groups *page 3 of 3*

WORKSHEET #7

Name: _____ Date: _____

Dov Gruner

TUVIA

DOV GRUNER (1912–1947) was born in Hungary. In 1940, he came to Israel on an *"Aliyah Bet"* ship and was captured by the British. He spent six months in the Atlit internment camp. In 1941, he joined the British army in order to fight the Nazis, and together with his comrades in the Jewish Brigade came to the aid of Holocaust survivors in Europe. He was decorated for his bravery. Dov learned that his entire Hungarian family had been murdered in the Holocaust, and that the British Mandate were cruelly enforcing their infamous 1939 White Paper limiting immigration and land purchase. Upon this discovery, he became a member of the Irgun and joined its fighting force. He was severely wounded in an attack on the Ramat Gan police station, subsequently caught by the British, and sentenced to death. He was thirty-five years old when he went to the gallows on April 16, 1947, after refusing to recognise the right of the British court to try him together with his comrades Mordechai Alkahi, Yechiel Dresner and Eliezer Kashani.

Dov Gruner wrote in a letter to his commander Menachem Begin:

"Of course I want to live. Who does not? But if I am sorry I'm about to 'finish' it is mainly because I did not manage to do enough. I too could have let the future fend for itself – taken the job I was promised or left the country and lived securely in America. But that would not have given me satisfaction as a Jew and certainly not as a Zionist… That should be the way of the Jewish people in these days, to stand up for what is ours and be ready for battle even if in some instances it leads to the gallows. I write these lines forty-eight hours before the time fixed by our oppressors to carry out their murder and at such moments one does not lie. I swear that if I had the choice of starting again I would choose the same road, regardless of the possible consequences to me."

Dov

Question:
What is your reaction to Dov's letter?

Name:_____   Date:_____

Orde Charles Wingate

"Judged by ordinary standards, [Wingate] would not be regarded as normal. But his own standards were far from ordinary. He was a military genius and a wonderful man."

– Moshe Dayan

TUVIA

ORDE CHARLES WINGATE (1903–1944) was born to a religious Christian family and was a firm believer in the Bible. He passionately embraced the prophetic vision of Jewish redemption and the Jews' ultimate return to the Land of Israel. During his service in the Land of Israel, he worked to help realise that ideal.

The son of a British officer, Wingate was born in India, received a a education and was commissioned in 1923. He served in India and then in the Sudan, where he studied Arabic and Semitics, and acquired a familiarity with the Middle East. Wingate was recognised as a talented officer, and by 1936 he had earned the rank of captain. That same year he was transferred to the British Mandate of Palestine, where he served for the next three years.

Wingate arrived in *Eretz Yisrael* as an intelligence officer at a time when small bands of Arab rioters were regularly attacking both the British and the Jews. To counter this offensive, Wingate organised and trained "Special Night Squads," comprised primarily of *Haganah* fighters, which were successfully employed throughout the *Yishuv*. Their tactics were based on the strategic principles of surprise, mobility and night attacks, and they served effectively both as defensive and offensive units, successfully pre-empting and resisting Arab attacks.

Wingate maintained good contacts with the heads of the *Yishuv* and the *Haganah*. He learned Hebrew, and he demonstrated his ardent belief that the Jews were entitled to their homeland in the Land of Israel. He also recognised the need for a working military force, and he dreamed of heading the army of the future Jewish state. Because of his efforts and support, he was called in the *Yishuv*, "*ha-yedid*," the friend.

Wingate's intense support for the Zionist viewpoint, however, was controversial. In 1939 the British succumbed to Arab pressure and transferred Wingate from the Land of Israel. His passport was stamped with the restriction that he not be allowed to re-enter the country. His personal involvement with the Zionist cause was thus curtailed, but many of those he trained became heads of the Palmach and, later, the Israel Defense Forces.

continued on next page

Wingate returned briefly to Great Britain, but, recognised for his military talent, he was transferred to further active duty. In 1941 he led the force in Ethiopia against the Italians and was a major figure in liberating the country. He then served in Burma, where he received the rank of Brigadier General, organising and training the Chindits, a special jungle unit that operated behind Japanese lines. Wingate was killed in an airplane crash in Burma in 1944 and is buried in Arlington National Cemetery in Virginia.

Wingate's friendship for the *Yishuv* and his contributions to its defense have been recognised through the several locations in Israel named for him, including the Wingate College of Physical Education near Netanya and Yemin Orde Youth Village.

> "There was a man of genius who might well
> have become also a man of destiny."
>
> – Winston Churchill

Postscript:
Inscription of Wingate's widow, Lorna Wingate, in the Bible she gave to the defenders of Yemin Orde (Ramat Naftali) in the War of Independence in 1948:

> "TO THE DEFENDERS OF YEMIN ORDE:
> 7/5/48
>
> Since Orde Wingate is with you in spirit, though he cannot lead you in the flesh; I send you the Bible he carried in all his campaigns, from which he drew the inspiration of his victories. Pray it be a covenant between you and him, in triumph or defeat, now and forever."

Question:
What lessons can we learn from the life of this Christian Zionist?

Orde Charles Wingate *page 2 of 2*

The State of Israel: War and Peace
(1948—present)

Part One: War —
"The Silver Platter"

MISCONCEPTION: The History of Israel is just one long string of aggressive, expansionist wars waged by the Jewish army with the ultimate aim of "occupying Arab land."

REALITY: The State of Israel has had to engage in a number of legitimate defensive wars in order to protect its population from threatened annihilation. Despite this reality, Israel has always reached out its hand for peace.

Objectives:

- Understand the importance of having a Jewish State and what it means to Jews all over the world.
- Comprehend that we did not receive the State "on a silver platter" (Chaim Weizman) but as a result of the heroic sacrifice of young men and women of the IDF.
- Survey the wars focusing on individual participants.
- Emphasise that Israel only wants peace. After each war Israel has always striven for peace with her enemies.

TUVIA

A: Introduction and Motivation

1. Remind the students: "During this course we have worked together on defining Zionism in the twenty-first century. We have to realise that the ultimate goal of Zionism was to establish a Jewish State in the Land of Israel. The big question is: "What happened after this dream became a reality on May 14th 1948?"

2. Israel's detractors would have one believe that there has been just one long series of wars and that the Jewish presence in the Middle East is a destabilising force in the world. While there have been wars of self-defense, which we will examine in this unit, Israel's rise out of the ashes like a phoenix is one of history's epics of human perseverance. In a relatively brief period of time, Israel has built a country that is a leader in many fields and a source of pride to Jews world over. We will be examining some of Israel's accomplishments in the next unit (Peace: "A Light unto the Nations").

3. Start the lesson by reading "The Silver Platter" by Natan Alterman (Worksheet #1) and discussing the questions on it.

B: The Wars

In order to examine Israel's conventional wars we need to chart a brief survey of the causes and results of the wars. We will examine the survey of the main conventional wars and significant anti-terror operations. The students should then make a chart with the following columns:

Name of Conflict and Year	Reasons for Outbreak	Results
War of Independence (1948–9)		
Sinai Campaign (1956)		
Six Day War (1967)		
Yom Kippur War (1973)		
Peace for Galilee/Lebanon (1982)		
Second Lebanon War (2006)		
Operation Cast Lead (2008–9)		
Operation Protective Edge (2014)		

Rather than examine each conventional war in detail, we will examine a summary of each conflict and study a participant of each war.

1. 1948 (Worksheet #2): We will read about David 'Mickey' Marcus (Worksheet #3), a volunteer American officer who played a vital role in opening the road to Jerusalem. (Suggestion: show a clip from "Cast a Giant Shadow," a film about David Marcus starring Kirk Douglas).

2. In the 1967 Six-Day War (Worksheet #5), we will look at the victory and read about Eli Cohen (Worksheet #6), a famous undercover agent who helped Israel achieve victory with the vital intelligence that he provided. (Suggestion: show the films: "Six Days in June" and/or "The Impossible Spy").

3. In 1973 (Worksheet #7), the tank battles in the Golan Heights helped save the Jewish State. We will learn about Avigdor Kahalani, one of the tank commanders.

4. In 1982 (Worksheet #8), Southern Lebanon was a PLO terrorist mini-state. After Israel successfully drove the PLO out, Israel had a military presence in a security zone until it finally withdrew in 2000. We will look at the writings of Alex Singer, an American volunteer in an Israeli combat unit who fell in Lebanon. (Suggestion: show the film "Alex – His Life in His Words and Drawings" [thirteen minutes]. Discuss the film with the students).

5. In 2006 (Worksheet #9) Southern Lebanon, once again, had become a terrorist mini-state, this time controlled by the Iranian-armed, Syrian-backed Terrorist group Hezbollah. After an unprovoked cross border attack followed by a missile barrage of Northern Israel Israel reacted by attempting to destroy the Hezbollah in the Second Lebanon War. The results of this war were inconclusive. In this conflict, as in Israel's other wars, a great many individual IDF soldiers displayed tremendous personal courage. We will study the life of Michael Levin. (Suggestion: Screen the film "A Hero in Heaven," followed by a discussion with the students.)

6. In December 2008 and July 2014 the IDF launched Operations Cast Lead and Protective Edge (Worksheet #10) in response to years of indiscriminate shelling of communities in southern Israel. The combined air, sea and ground operations had, by their conclusions largely achieved their aim of allowing the citizens of Israel to live in peace.

C: Conclusion

The War of Independence began in 1947 with the Arabs' rejection of the UN Partition Plan (Resolution 181), and concluded with the armistice agreements signed in Rhodes in 1949. Despite the overwhelming military advantages of the invading Arab states, the Jewish state, battling for its first breaths of air, managed to survive and eventually flourish. In 1967 the impartial observer would not have rated Israel's chances of survival very highly. There were overwhelming forces massed on all of its fragile borders. Yet within six days, a "modern miracle" occurred and the tables were turned. In 1973, although Egypt and Syria had the advantages of surprise and superior Soviet weaponry, Israel once again prevailed because of the *dvekut* (perseverance) of our people to the dream of an independent Jewish Homeland.

Stress that after each war Israel reached out her hand for peace. Finally Egypt, after trying to defeat Israel three times on the field of battle, realised that the only way to get what it wanted was through peaceful negotiations. In 1979, the Camp David accords gave Egypt the entire Sinai Peninsula and dismantled all the Israeli settlements and military bases in return for recognising the Jewish State and making peace. In 1994, Jordan followed the Egyptian precedent. Israel has been trying to make peace with the PLO since the 1993 Oslo accords. The Arab world must realise that they will never achieve peace through war and terror but only through peaceful negotiation and recognition of the Jewish State.

The individuals we studied helped to make this dream a reality. Ask the students who inspired them most, and why? We must all strive to make Israel a better place just as these heroic individuals did. That does not necessarily mean going into the battlefield. What ways can you think of to preserve and perfect the dream?

"A state is not handed to a people on a silver platter"

(Chaim Weizman)

"אין מדינה ניתנת לעם
אלא על מגש של כסף"

(חיים וייצמן)

Name: _____   Date: _____

The Silver Platter

"A state is not handed
to a people on a silver platter."
(Chaim Weizman, first President of Israel)

So the land grows still.
Red fades in the sky
Over smoking borders.
Heartsick but breathing, the people greet
The miracle that has no parallel.

Beneath the moon, they stand and wait,
Facing the dawn in awe and joy;
Then slowly towards the waiting throng
Two step forth – a girl and a boy.

Clad for work and for war, heavy shod and still,
Up the winding path they make their way,
Their clothes unchanged, still soiled with the grime
Of the battle-filled night and the toilsome day.

Weary past telling, strangers to sleep,
But wearing their youth like dew in their hair,
Mute they approach. – Are they living or dead?
Who knows, as they stand unmoving there.

Tear-stained, wondering, the people ask,
"Who are you?" – softly reply the two,
"We are the silver platter, on which
The Jewish State is handed you!"

In shadow they fall when their tale is told –
The rest let Israel's story unfold.

– Natan Alterman

"אין מדינה ניתנת לעם
על מגש של כסף."
(חיים ויצמן ,נשיאה הראשון של ישראל)

והארץ תשקוט, עין שמיים אודמת
תעמעם לאיטה
על גבולות עשנים
ואומה תעמוד – קרועת לב אך נושמת...
לקבל את הנס
האחד, אין שני...

היא לטקס תכון, היא תקום למול הסהר
ועמדה טרם יום עוטה חג ואימה.
– אז מנגד יצאו
נערה ונער
ואט אט יצעדו הם אל מול האומה.

לובשי חול וחגור, וכבדי נעליים
בנתיב יעלו הם
הלוך והחרש
לא החליפו בגדם, לא מחו עוד במים
את עקבות יום הפרך וליל קו האש.

עייפים עד בלי קץ, נזירים ממרגוע
ונוטפים טללי נעורים עבריים –
דום השניים יגשו
ועמדו לבלי נוע
ואין אות אם חיים הם או אם ירויים.

אז תשאל האומה שטופת דמע וקסם
ואמרה: "מי אתם?", והשניים שוקטים
יענו לה: "אנחנו מגש הכסף,
שעליו לך נתנה מדינת היהודים".

כך יאמרו ונפלו לרגליה עוטפי צל
והשאר יסופר בתולדות ישראל.

– נתן אלתרמן

Questions:

1. What does Chaim Weizman's statement mean?
2. What were your feelings when you read this poem?
3. Who are "the silent two?"
4. What is the meaning of the last stanza?
5. What would be an appropriate time to recite this poem?

91

Name:_____ Date:_____

The War of Independence (1947–1949)

The War of Independence lasted from the end of November 1947 until July 1949. The war was divided into two distinct phases.

The first phase began on November 30, the day after the UN General Assembly adopted its resolution on the partition of Palestine (Map One), and ended on May 15, 1948, the last day of the British Mandate.

1. The 1947 United Nations Partition Plan, accepted by the Jews but rejected by the Arabs.

The second phase started on the very last day of the British Mandate and came to an end on July 20,1949, when the last of the Armistice Agreements (with Syria) was signed (Map Two).

In the first phase which began on the morrow of the UN Partition Resolution, the *Yishuv* (Palestinian Jews) and its defense forces were under attack by Palestinian Arabs, aided by irregular volunteers from Arab countries. On May 14, 1948, the day preceding the end of British Mandate, the National Council convened at the Tel Aviv Museum and approved the Proclamation of Independence, which declared the establishment of the State of Israel.

During the night of May 14–15, Egyptian airplanes bombarded Tel Aviv. Thus began the second phase of the War of Independence, in which the regular armies of five neighboring Arab states invaded the new state of Israel. From the north, east and south came the armies of Lebanon, Syria, Iraq, Transjordan and Egypt. (Saudi Arabia sent a formation to fight under Egyptian command. Yemen considered itself at war with Israel but sent no military forces.)

The War of Independence lasted for more than thirteen months. Israel paid a heavy price: 4000 soldiers and 2000 civilians killed (1% of the entire population). The financial cost was heavy as well. The Jewish State, however, was now a definite fact. It held an area of almost 8000 square miles compared with some 6200 square miles granted within the boundaries as drawn up in the Partition Plan.

2. The armistice lines of 1949

WORKSHEET #3

Name: _____   Date: _____

David Marcus: American Jew – *Gibor Yisrael* [Israeli Hero]
by Yossi Katz

TUVIA

COLONEL DAVID MARCUS (1902–1948) was a real American success story. He rose out of the slums of New York City to become an all – American athlete, a Rhodes scholar and an officer in the United States Army. After completing law school at night, David went on to become a successful attorney and later a respected judge with a bright future. In 1948 Marcus left all the comforts and promises of life in America to join the Jewish people struggling for independence in Israel. It was there that he would attain his greatest achievement and meet a tragic death in the hills of Jerusalem.

David "Mickey" Marcus was born on Washington's Birthday In 1902 (February 22), the fifth child of poor Jewish immigrants from Romania. The family lived on Hester Street in New York's Lower East Side and later moved to Brooklyn. Mickey's parents had high hopes for him and he seemed destined from an early age to fulfill their wish. David Marcus graduated at the top of his high school class and was voted Best Athlete. He received high school letters in track, basketball, baseball and football. A member of the scholastic Honour Society, Mickey could have gone to any college in America, but his inner convictions led him to a decision that shocked his family and friends. In 1920, David Marcus became one of the few Jews to enter the United States Military Academy at West Point. Cadet Marcus showed an exceptional aptitude for the military sciences and excelled in all his studies. During his junior year Mickey took up boxing and went on undefeated to take the U.S. Intercollegiate Boxing Championship. In his senior year Marcus concentrated on gymnastics and won several national titles as well as an invitation to try out for the 1924 U.S. Olympic Team. Mickey graduated from West Point in 1924 at the top of his class and was offered a Rhodes scholarship to Oxford University in England. He declined the offer in order to be near his sweetheart, Emma, whom he married in 1927.

After getting married, Mickey left the army and completed night law school. He quickly made a name for himself as a competent lawyer, first serving in the U.S. Attorney General Office and later on the New York Commission of Corrections. In 1936 he was appointed to the Bench and in 1940 Mayor Fiorello LaGuardia named him Commissioner of Corrections. It was in that capacity that Mickey made national headlines with his successful war on organised crime and corruption.

When World War II broke out, David Marcus temporarily left his promising career to re-enlist in the Army. As a West Point graduate, Colonel Marcus was appointed Commander of the Rangers Training School in Oahu. On D-Day he volunteered to parachute into Normandy with the 101st Airborne despite he fact that he had never received any training as a paratrooper. His courage and heroics won for him several major United States and British

continued on next page

decorations including the Distinguished Service Metal. In 1945 Colonel Marcus took part in the liberation of Dachau Concentration Camp and it was there that he witnessed the horrors of the Nazi Holocaust. Haunted by what he had seen, Marcus became convinced of the need for a Jewish homeland in Israel. In 1947 Mickey retired from the Army and resumed his legal practice in New York.

On November 29, 1947 the United Nations voted in favor of establishing an independent Jewish State in Palestine. The very next day Arab terrorists opened fire on a Jewish bus traveling to Jerusalem, in effect beginning the War of Independence. Palestinian Arabs sought to isolate and harass Jewish settlements including Jerusalem in anticipation of the British evacuation, which would be several months away. The local Arabs hoped that regular armies from the surrounding Arab countries would invade and destroy the newborn Jewish State. David Ben Gurion, leader of the Jewish *Yishuv* in Israel and later the State's first Prime Minister, understood the gravity of the situation. The Jewish army was out-gunned, out-manned and ill prepared.

Ben Gurion sent an emissary to the United States to recruit an American Jewish army officer who would be willing to help build a new strong Israeli armed force capable of securing and maintaining independence. As Ben Gurion later said, "there were many who could have come, but only one came!" That person was David Marcus. Leaving a comfortable life, a promising career and a devoted wife behind, Marcus arrived in Israel on January 1948 under the *nom de guerre* Mickey Stone. Serving as Ben Gurion's personal military advisor, Mickey quickly perceived the special spirit and needs of the new army. He prepared vital military manuals, improved training procedures and made important observations and recommendations. Using his vast military expertise, David Marcus helped mold Israel's scattered underground forces into a modern army. After a brief visit to the U.S., Mickey returned to Israel in May of 1948.

Minutes after declaring independence on May 14, Israel was invaded by five Arab armies. The most critical battle areas proved to be in the south (Negev) along the Egyptian line of invasion, up the coast, and in the Judean Hills where the Arab Legion laid siege to Jerusalem. Mickey devoted all of his energy and talent to relieving those two fronts. In the Negev Mickey organised a special mechanised unit that fought out of jeeps and armoured half-trucks known as the "Beasts of the Negev". This unit succeeded in halting the Egyptian advance and helped raise the fighting spirit of the Jewish troops. Marcus' greatest challenge, however, was to be in the hills of Jerusalem.

On May 28 the Jewish Quarter in the Old City of Jerusalem surrendered to the Arab legion. At the same time Arab soldiers succeeded in cutting off the road to the New City of Jerusalem, in effect putting a stranglehold on 85,000 Jews. Physically isolated but spiritually inseparable for the rest of Israel, Jerusalem's destiny held the key to the young State's future. Realising the need from strong and united leadership, Ben-Gurion appointed David Marcus Supreme Commander of the Jerusalem Front with the rank of *Aluf* (Hebrew for General). Marcus became the first Jew since Judah the Macabee to hold this rank in Israel.

David Marcus: American Jew – *Gibor Yisrael* [Israeli Hero] *page 2 of 3*

WORKSHEET #3

Aluf Marcus knew that his primary objective was to break the Arab siege of Jerusalem, but charred armoured vehicles lining the road to the Holy City stood as grim reminders of those who had failed in previous attempts. Aware of this, Mickey turned his attention towards finding an alternative route.

In late May, three Israeli soldiers on leave descended on foot from Jerusalem to Tel Aviv and discovered an old goat path that ran parallel to the blocked main highway. Marcus began to infiltrate troops and supplies by foot along this trail and speculated that the path might be widened to enable vehicles to pass through. With a United Nations truce days away, Marcus brought in hundreds of laborers from the coast who began clearing boulders and dynamiting rock sidings. If the road were not completed by June 11 (the day the truce went into effect), no further work would be permitted and Jerusalem would starve. Under Mickey's brilliant leadership, the "Burma Road" was completed and on June 9th the first trucks loaded with water, food and supplies entered Jerusalem. There, they were greeted by thousands of the city's grateful citizens. David Marcus had saved Jerusalem.

Sadly, Mickey's heroic life was to have a tragic end. Mickey was waiting outside his headquarters near Abu-Ghosh when the Jewish sentry, on the watch for Arab terrorists, challenged the figure in the dark. When Mickey answered in English, the frightened sentry fired a shot, killing Marcus instantly. Mickey was the last casualty on the Jerusalem front before the truce began on June 11.

David Marcus, hero of Israel, was buried at West Point's Military Cemetery with full military honors. In a letter to his bereaved wife Emma, David Ben Gurion stated the Jewish nation's feeling in simple words, "He was the best man we had." *

Postscript: In a letter to his wife Marcus wrote, "I doubt if I have ever done anything – anywhere – any time, that is more worthwhile."

Questions:
1. Why did David Marcus leave his home and wife to volunteer to fight for Israel?
2. David was one of many "*Machalnikim*" (volunteers from outside Israel) to fight in the War of Independence. What does this teach us about the concept of a Jewish Homeland?
3. Point for discussion: If you were a college student and you heard that Israel was, once again, facing a war for survival, would you drop everything and come to Israel? If so, what would you do there? If not, why not?

---

* Yossi Katz, *A Voice Called, Stories of Jewish Heroism*, (Gefen: Jerusalem/New York, 2010/5770).

David Marcus: American Jew – *Gibor Yisrael* [Israeli Hero] *page 3 of 3*

Name: _____   Date: _____

Sinai Campaign (1956)

The Sinai Campaign, also known as "Operation Kadesh," lasted eight days from October 29, 1956 to November 5, 1956. The short war between Israel and Egypt partly coincided with the Anglo-French Suez Campaign. The Sinai Campaign was launched by Israel as a reaction to the increasing Fedayeen terror activities resulting in the murders of hundreds of Israeli civilians. The Anglo-French attack on Egypt came as a result of Egypt's nationalisation of the Suez Canal.

The objectives of Israel's operation were:
- Destruction of the Fedayeen terror bases in the Gaza Strip and on the Sinai border.
- Prevention of an Egyptian attack on Israel by destroying Egypt's logistic establishment and airfields in Sinai.
- Opening the Gulf of Eilat to Israeli shipping.

By November 5, 1956, the Israeli Army captured the Sinai Peninsula, Gaza Strip and Sharm el-Sheikh. IDF losses in the campaign were 171 dead, several hundred wounded, and four Israelis taken as prisoners. Egyptian losses were estimated at several thousand dead and wounded, and 6,000 prisoners taken.

As a result of a prolonged political struggle, in which both the United States and the Soviet Union opposed Israel, the IDF was compelled to evacuate the Sinai Peninsula and the Gaza Strip. Troops of the United Nations Emergency Force (UNEF) were posted in the Gaza Strip and Sharm el-Sheikh to guarantee free passage of Israeli shipping through the Straits of Tiran. Israel secured a considerable degree of quiet on its southwestern border and open access to Eilat. These gains were preserved until 1967.

Questions:
How do you think Israel felt when...

1. Both of the super-powers (U.S.A. and U.S.S.R.) forced it to evacuate all the recently hard-won territory for a fragile agreement that was broken by Egypt within a decade?
2. In 1967 the world stood by and did nothing, despite the fact that they had agreed to come to Israel's aid when the agreement was broken?

Name:_____ Date:_____

The Six-Day War (1967)

- On May 15, 1967, Egyptian military forces moved into the Sinai. On May 17 the Egyptian President, Nasser, demanded the withdrawal of the UN Emergency Force. They withdrew without protest.
- On May 22, Nasser declared the Straits of Tiran closed to shipping bound to and from Israel. There was no reaction from the iternational community, despite a signed treaty.
- On the 25th, Iraq and Saudi Arabia moved their troops to Israel's border.
- On May 26, Nasser declared that this time the intention was to destroy Israel.
- On May 30, Jordan signed a pact with Egypt.
- On June 4, Iraq signed a similar agreement.
- On the morning of June 5, the Israeli Air Force undertook a preemptive attack designed to destroy the Arab air forces and their airfields. In fewer than three hours, this objective was achieved. On the same morning, Israel Southern Command moved its forces in Sinai. By the end of the fourth day, the war in Sinai was over.
- Israel had captured the entire Sinai Peninsula and the Gaza Strip.
- The Straits of Tiran were opened.

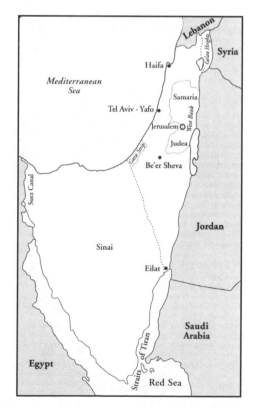

The cease-fire lines after the Six-Day War of 1967

continued on next page

On the morning of June 5, Israel had notified King Hussein that if his forces kept the peace, Jordan would be immune to attack. Nevertheless, Jordanian forces opened fire almost immediately all along the armistice line and shelled western Jerusalem. After a second warning was ignored, Israel Central Command counter-attacked.

On June 7, the Old City of Jerusalem was taken by a paratroop unit who fought hand-to-hand in order to avoid any damage to the holy places. By the evening, the whole of Judea and Samaria (called the West Bank by the Jordanians) was in Israel's hands.

In the north, the Syrians had been shelling Israel's towns and villages from their heavily fortified positions on the Golan Heights. With the fighting over in the south and the center, The Israeli Defense Forces attacked the Syrian army on June 9. By June 10, Israeli forces had captured the Golan Heights and the constant danger of Syrian shelling had been removed from the Israel villages and kibbutzim.

With the acceptance of the cease-fire by all parties, the Six-Day War came to an end. Israeli casualties were 777 killed and 2,586 wounded. The Arabs had lost some 15,000 men.

The Wars Aftermath and UN Resolution 242

The Six Day War concluded with UN Resolution 242, which called for an Israeli withdrawal, without specifying the lines of that withdrawal: "Withdrawal of Israel armed forces from territories occupied in the recent conflict," and for the, "termination of all claims or states of belligerency and respect for and acknowledgement of the sovereignty, territorial integrity and political independence of every State in the area and their right to live in peace within secure and recognized boundaries free from threats or acts of force."

After the 1967 Six-Day War, Israel was – in Defense Minister Moshe Dayan's famous phrase – "waiting for a telephone call" from Arab leaders. Israelis expected to hear that now, at last, their neighbours were ready to talk peace. Having escaped not only feared annihilation, but also winning a seemingly miraculous victory, Israel's leaders did two things: They vowed not to return to the vulnerable armistice lines of 1948 and '49 or to a divided Jerusalem, and yet to be "unbelievably generous in working out peace terms," as Foreign Minister Abba Eban put it. In direct talks with Arab countries, "everything is negotiable," he said.

However, following the war, the leaders of thirteen Arab states gathered at a summit conference in Khartoum, Sudan. There they pledged to continue their struggle against Israel. Influenced by the Egyptian leader, Nasser, their conditions were quite specific: no peace with Israel, no negotiations with Israel, no recognition of Israel. *

Questions:

1. What do you think the feeling was throughout the Jewish world in May 1967?
2. What were the results of the Six-Day war physically, emotionally and psychologically?
3. What is the significance of the wording of UN Resolution 242?
4. How does the legacy of the Six-Day War affect the region today?

---

* Adapted from, http://www.camera.org

The Six Day War *page 2 of 2*

Eli Cohen: The Undercover Warrior

By former Prime Minister Yitzhak Shamir

TUVIA

It was 1965 – two years before the Six Day War, which led Israel to its highest military, political, and economic achievements and earned it enormous prestige around the world and in Jewish communities.

As often happens during drastic changes, the period of dazzling success was preceded by gray and sad times. Israel was burdened with grave defense and economic difficulties. There was a pervasive sense of gloom.

The year 1965 did not bring much hope. One day in May, Israel was shocked by the report that an Israeli had been executed in Damascus in the middle of the night. His body was put on display, wrapped in a white sheet inscribed with a list of the amazing crimes of espionage he had committed for Israel. Syrian, Lebanese and other Arab newspapers were full of wondrous stories about the legendary achievements of the Israeli spy who had arrived in Damascus from Tel Aviv and, for four years, had provided the Israeli enemy with Syria's most classified and important security secrets.

According to the Arab press, Eli Cohen was born in Alexandria, Egypt in 1924. His parents had emigrated there from Syria. He was an excellent student at the Jewish school and studied engineering at the Farouk University. He immigrated to Israel in 1957 and settled in Bat Yam. He worked as an accountant, married an immigrant from Iraq named Nadia, had children and lived a quiet family life until friends and associates learned about his character and talents. He joined the Israeli Intelligence Service in the early 1960s.

He was trained as an agent and, in 1961, his commanders decided to build a cover story for him. He was to pose as an Arab who had been born in Lebanon, immigrated to Argentina and had decided to return to the Middle East. He was sent to Argentina where he received an ID card identifying him as Kamal Amin Tabat, a businessman. Quite easily, Cohen befriended several Arabs of Lebanese and Syrian origin and made a name for himself as a successful and serious man, who cared about the Arab cause, was an earnest supporter of the Syrian Ba'ath party, and wished to settle in Syria.

Cohen arrived in Damascus in 1962. He rented an apartment in a luxurious part of the Syrian capital and established a reputation as a successful businessman. He befriended mainly military men with whom he traveled all over the country. He had many friends, including some very prominent ones who spent time with him in his handsome apartment in an ambiance of carefree luxury. He gleaned extensive and valuable information from conversations with his friends which helped him answer queries from his Israeli commanders. The newspapers said that while he lived in Damascus, he sent hundreds of messages to Israel, thus enabling his operators to form a correct and balanced analysis of the situation in Syria. He used to travel on business to Europe every six months where he met his contacts and

Eli Cohen: The Undercover Warrior *page 3 of 3*

received both money for expenses and instructions for future activities. During these trips, he also visited his growing family in Bat Yam.

This routine of taking short trips to Europe and going on brief visits home must have been difficult for him. His wife Nadia said that during his last visit, he was sad and nervous. Undoubtedly aware of the risks he had been taking, he nevertheless decided to continue his double life and returned to Damascus. It may be assumed that his operators had told him he was doing well, although, as the story goes, he had been warned not to make too many transmissions, as these might expose his activities.

The Arab papers said that Cohen's lifestyle and multiple contacts with the military eventually made the Syrian security services suspect him, and they started following him.

There are various accounts of how he was caught. According to several sources, he was picked up by a radio detector and caught while transmitting to Israel. At first, he tried to deny his identity and mission but, after being subjected to severe torture, he revealed his modus operandi and even told his interrogators of the orders he had received on his last trip. It is said that the Syrians tried to force him to continue communicating with Israel but following a prearranged stratagem, he managed to inform his operators that he had been caught.

His interrogation and trial lasted three months. He was hanged on the 18th of May 1965. Before he was executed, he was allowed to meet the Rabbi of Damascus and send a letter to his wife in which he asked her to remarry so that his children would have someone to take care of them. His Israeli operators went to great lengths to rescue him and the best French lawyers were hired, but they were not allowed to meet with him. Syria was offered large sums of money, and prominent international figures and organisations intervened on his behalf, but all to no avail.

Many years have passed since then. The Israeli public will forever remember Cohen as an honest and serious man who was devoted to his people and his country, and who operated with a deep conviction that he was serving his nation despite enormous but necessary risks. The image of his body dangling from a rope is etched in the hearts of many Israelis, and his name is spoken with reverence.

There are few like him in the Israeli Hall of Fame. Many heroes fought their people's enemies courageously, but few were spies, undercover warriors, who constantly risked their lives in solitude, conducting a war of the mind. Eli Cohen's name will live forever in the memory of the people.

Speaking in an interview with a Syrian Reporter 24 hours before his execution, Eli Cohen said: "I went to Syria on a mission from the Israeli intelligence to secure a future for my wife, my children and my family."

WORKSHEET #6

Shaul Cohen's Bar Mitzvah Speech

Eli's son, Shaul, was only two weeks old when his father last saw him. At Kfar Habad, on July 29, 1977 at the Bar Mitzvah for 100 fatherless boys, Shaul was asked to say something on their behalf. This is what he said:

"I would like to have been like all other children. I would have liked my father to be a simple man and not a hero. Then he would be alive and I would have had a father whom I knew, and who lived with us like all other fathers.

I have read everything about my father's life and what he did for our country. I have collected all the books, articles and photographs. But I have hesitated to talk about him until now for I knew that it still hurt my mother when my father's name was mentioned. I will now make my vow. I promise, you, father, that in my life I will never fail you. I will do my duty with all my strength and devotion for the State of Israel. I will be a faithful son of an admired hero. I will try to be like you, father. That's my pledge."

TUVIA

Questions:
1. How did you react to the story of Eli Cohen?
2. What do you think of Shaul's speech?
3. What is the meaning of the following line: "I will try to be like you, father"?

Eli Cohen: The Undercover Warrior *page 3 of 3*

Name: _____ Date: _____

The Yom Kippur War (October 1973)

The Yom Kippur War began on October 6, 1973 on the Jewish Day of Atonement and was the fiercest Arab-Israeli war since the War of Independence in 1948. Egypt and Syria attacked Israel, catching Israel off guard.

Committing the cardinal sin of warfare, Israeli Intelligence and strategic planners underestimated their enemy, convincing themselves that the Arabs lacked the ability to alter their combat methods.

Egyptian forces crossed the Suez Canal at five points and Syrian forces attacked at two points on the Golan Heights.

On the northern front:

Israeli troops pushed the Syrians back to the cease-fire line by October 10 despite the arrival of Iraqi troops to support the Syrians. By October 12, the Israelis had advanced to within 40 kilometers of Damascus.

On the southern front:

In the course of the first days of the war, Egyptian troops forced the Israelis to give up the "Bar Lev Defense Line" on the east bank of the Suez Canal. On October 16, Israel sent a task force across the Suez Canal to attack Egyptian tanks, missile sites, and artillery on the West Bank. Within a few days, Israeli forces were at the outskirts of the city of Ismailiya and some 100 kilometers from Cairo.

In the later stages of the Yom Kippur War, after Israel repulsed the Syrian attack on the Golan Heights and established a bridgehead on the Egyptian side of the Suez Canal, international efforts to end the fighting were intensified. On October 20, the U.S. Secretary of State, Henry Kissinger, flew to Moscow, and – together with the Soviet government – the U.S. proposed a cease-fire resolution in the UN Security Council. On October 24, 1973, the cease-fire went into effect, thus ending the fighting. Despite committing huge strategic and doctrinal errors, the IDF prevailed, thanks in no small part to the courage, initiative and combat skills of its soldiers, particularly its elite armour crews and commanders.

During eighteen days of fighting, Israel casualties were more than 2,500 killed. Egypt lost 7,500 soldiers and Syria lost 7,300.

Questions:
1. How do you think this affected Israel's image at home and abroad?
2. What were the initial results of this war?
3. Would the first Camp David peace agreement with Egypt have been possible without this war?

continued on next page

WORKSHEET #7

AVIGDOR KAHALANI

TUVIA

AVIGDOR KAHALANI (1944–) is the son of Immigrants from Yemen. Despite having received horrific burns in his tank during the Six-Day War, he volunteered to stay in the Tank Corps and became a Battalion Commander.

On the fourth day of battle in the Yom Kippur War, the Syrians launched a new and formidable attack from a valley north of Kuneitra. In a major assault, hundreds of modern Arab tanks began moving up from the bottom of the valley hoping to take higher ground. By then, Israeli forces in the northern Golan were able to field only about 40 operational tanks against 500 Syrian tanks. Had they gained access to the plateau, they would have been able to spread out their forces and control the central Golan Heights. From there, it would have been easy to penetrate even deeper into Israel and potentially cut Israel into two. The lone force standing between the Syrians and Israel's possible destruction was the IDF's 77th Armoured Battalion, known as Oz 77, under the command of 29-year-old Lt. Col. Avigdor Kahalani.

Kahalani was sent to the valley in a last-ditch effort to stem the Syrian advance. Calling his men to join him in a rush towards the enemy, he was shocked to find that a commander's worst nightmare had come true: he was moving forward alone. Physically and emotionally at the end of their rope, the men had simply not responded.

When Kahalani's tank reached the crest of the hill, he found himself face-to-face with three Syrian tanks. Incredibly, his crew managed to destroy first one tank then another a mere fifty meters away. As a third tank aimed its cannon in Kahalani's direction, his guns jammed. Nevertheless, the Syrian tank burst into flames, hit by Israel troops who had finally rallied to his support. The battle raged all day long until the Syrians, who suffered their own heavy losses, finally retreated, leaving behind 260 wrecked tanks, 500 armoured personnel carriers and numerous other vehicles. The burning smoking hulks littered the battlefield that would become known as *Emek Ha-Bacha* – The Valley of Tears.

The surviving tankers of the 7th Armoured Brigade had been in combat for more than 50 straight hours. For his actions, Oz 77 Commander Kahalani was awarded the Medal of Valour, Israel's highest combat decoration.

General Rafael Eitan said in an address to soldiers of the Armoured Corps after the war:

> "If we had not stopped the Syrians on the Golan Heights, then the State of Israel would have been destroyed...This division saved Israel from defeat, from catastrophe...I want to stress and make it clear to you; you saved the people of Israel. First and foremost, you!"

The Yom Kippur War *page 2 of 2*

WORKSHEET #8

Name:_____   Date:_____

Operation Peace for the Galilee (The Lebanon War) – June 1982

After the Six-Day War, most of the terrorist activities of the Palestinian Liberation Organisation (PLO) were carried out from Jordanian territory. In September 1970, there were fierce clashes between the PLO and the Jordanian army as a result of which thousands of Palestinians were killed and the organisation was expelled from Jordan.

After expulsion from Jordan, the main center for PLO terror became Southern Lebanon. The Lebanese government was unable to prevent terrorist activities. In 1978 Palestinians guerrillas launched an air raid on Israel from their bases in Lebanon. In retaliation, Israel sent troops into southern Lebanon to occupy a strip 6–10 kilometers deep and thus protect Israel's border (Litani Operation). Eventually, a UN peacekeeping force was set up.

In spite of the presence of the UN peacekeeping force, attacks against Israel continued. On June 6, 1982, Israel launched a massive attack to destroy all military bases of the PLO in Southern Lebanon and free Israel's northern towns and villages from constant fire. A ten-week siege of the Muslim sector of West Beirut, a PLO stronghold, forced the Palestinians to accept a U.S.-sponsored plan, whereby the PLO terrorists would evacuate Beirut and relocate to several Arab countries that had agreed to accept them. Israel withdrew from most of Lebanon in 1985, but continued to maintain a Lebanese buffer zone north of its border until its final unilateral withdrawal in 2000.

ALEXANDER SINGER

ALEXANDER SINGER (1962–1987), a Lieutenant in the Israel Defense Forces, was killed in action while on patrol in Lebanon. Alex is buried in Mt. Herzl Military Cemetery in Jerusalem.

Alex, a platoon commander who made *Aliyah* from America in 1984, was killed while trying to reach his commander whom he believed was wounded in a terrorist ambush. In fact, his commander had died instantly. When Alex, under fire, reached his commander he too was attacked and killed – on his 25th birthday. Another soldier, who then tried to reach the two of them, was also killed.

TUVIA

continued on next page

WORKSHEET #8

Alex, a *summa cum laude* graduate of Cornell University, was a writer, an artist, a lover of Zion, a yearner for peace and an observant Jew. He died while doing what he very much wanted to be doing. Among his journals the following poem, written while Alex was on the IDF officer training course, was found:

> Once in a while
> As I progress towards the course's end
> I feel a pang of fear.
>
> If the war comes,
> When the war comes
> I will have to lead men to die.
>
> But those men were not men a short time ago.
> Some don't even shave yet.
> And I will have to have the calm power
> To yell to them
> Or to whisper
>
> Kadima (Forward)
>
> And,
> I will have to have the calm power
> To step forward myself. *

Questions:

1. What were your thoughts after having seen the film and having read about Alex?
2. What meaning do you think the last stanza of the poem holds for us?
3. Point for Discussion: Alex's life personified the statement by Gandhi: "We must become the change we wish to see!" What change would you like to see and how would you have 'the calm power to step forward yourself' as Alex did?

---

* Singer, Alex, *Alex: Building A Life – The Story of an American Who Fell Defending Israel*, (Gefen: New York/Jerusalem, 1996)

Operation Peace for the Galilee *page 2 of 2*

Name:_____ Date:_____

The Second Lebanon War (2006)

The Second Lebanon War began on July 12, 2006 when Hezbollah, the Iranian-backed Lebanese Shiite terrorist organization, crossed the Lebanese border into Israel, killed several Israeli soldiers, and kidnapped two reserve soldiers.

Hezbollah also fired rockets and missiles on Israel's northern cities, attacks that were directed against toward the Israeli civilian population centers and exacted a terrible toll on lives and property.

Over one million Israelis lived in bomb shelters and about 300,000 temporarily left their homes and sought refuge in the south.

The Israel Defense Forces (IDF) response was an attempt to destroy the Hezbollah presence in what had essentially become a terror state in Southern Lebanon on Israel's northern border.

The IDF was hampered by both ethical and moral dilemmas relating to trying to root out Hezbollah terrorists who were deliberately embedded in the local civilian population, and the lack of a clear plan from the political leadership and the IDF General Staff.

The end of military operations was on August 14, 2006, with the passage of United Nations Security Council Resolution (UNSCR) 1701.

Despite the failures of planning, the individual IDF soldiers on the ground demonstrated tremendous bravery. 121 soldiers paid the ultimate sacrifice for their country. Two stories of heroism that emerged from the war that are particularly poignant are; Major Roi Klein (1975–2006) who jumped on a live grenade, after shouting *Shema Yisrael*, in order to save his fellow soldiers . He left behind a widow and two young children, and Michael Levin (1984–2006), the only Israeli/American soldier killed in the conflict.

Photo by Tuvia Book

"Milluim, A Band of Brothers"

continued on next page

MICHAEL LEVIN

TUVIA

MICHAEL LEVIN (1984–2006) was one of three soldiers killed on August 1, 2006 in clashes with Hezbollah in the southern Lebanese village of Aita al-Shaab. An immigrant from the United States, he had been living in Israel for the last four years.

Born and raised near Philadelphia, Pennsylvania, Michael grew up in a traditional, loving Jewish household. In February of 2001, Michael came to Israel for two months and attended the Alexander Muss High School in Israel (AMHSI) program. After graduating high school, Michael attended the NATIV USY year long program in Israel. In his NATIV yearbook he wrote:

You can't fulfill your dreams unless you dare to risk it all.

At the young age of 16, Michael had decided that he wanted to move to Israel and join a front-line combat unit in the Israeli Defense Forces. He followed his dream three years later, and immigrated to Israel, joining the elite paratroop unit #890 shortly thereafter. He served as a *Chayal Boded* (a "Lone Soldier," a volunteer for the IDF without family in Israel). In the summer of 2006 Michael had received special permission to travel to the United States to visit his family. When he heard about the outbreak of the war, he decided to end his trip and return to help his unit. He went straight to his commanders and demanded to be sent up north to defend Israel against Hezbollah. Seven days later he was killed. On Tisha B'Av, Michael Levin (z"l) was laid to rest at Mount Herzl Military Cemetery in Jerusalem. Michael's family was joined by thousands of people from all over Israel who came to pay tribute to his memory and his heroism.*

To honour Michael and all the "Lone Soldiers," his family and many friends, together with other former "Lone Soldiers" have opened four Lone Soldier Centers in memory of Michael Levin (http://lonesoldiercenter.com). The centers operate from branches in Jerusalem, Tel Aviv and Haifa. They provide many useful services to lone soldiers such as, helping to finding housing, providing furniture, organising Shabbat and holiday meals and counseling and most importantly a place to feel at home.

Questions:

1. What were the ideals Michael and other Lone Soldiers are willing to risk their lives for?
2. Why did so many people, most of whom did not know Michael, come to his funeral?
3. What were the goals of the IDF in the 2006 war in Lebanon? Were they achieved?

---

* Adapted from: http://www.aheroinheaven.com

The Second Lebanon War (2006) *page 2 of 2*

Name:_____ Date:_____

Operation Cast Lead (2008–2009) and Operation Protective Edge (2014)

After sustaining three years of rocket bombardment against its civilian population, Israel's leaders finally decided that a military response was necessary to defend its people. They had learned the lessons of the Second Lebanon War, and this time had a clear two-stage plan that had largely achieved its aims by the conclusion of the operation.

Background: Since the Israeli unilateral and complete disengagement from the Gaza Strip in 2005, approximately 5,700 rockets and 4,000 mortar shells had been fired from Gaza into Israel. Hamas terrorists fired over 2,000 rockets and 1,600 mortar shells in 2008 alone.

Stage 1: Israeli Air and Naval Forces struck Hamas terrorist cell headquarters throughout the Gaza Strip. They also attacked rocket launchers and Grad missile stockpiles. Houses of senior Hamas and Jihad terrorists were targeted along with dozens of tunnels that have been used to pass weaponry into Gaza.

Stage 2: On January 3, the IDF moved into Gaza in a ground operation. Operation Cast Lead successfully destroyed hundreds of terrorist enclaves, rocket launching pads and Hamas operative headquarters in Gaza allowing Israeli citizens in southern Israel to once again live normal lives without the constant threat of terror. No other army in the world has ever gone to the measures the IDF used so as to protect innocent lives.

In the summer of 2014 Israel initiated Operation Protective Edge in response to the persistent rockets being fired upon civilian populations in Israel. From the beginning of the operation in July through August, over 4,300 rockets were fired at Israel by Hamas and other terrorist groups in Gaza. IDF soldiers aided by the "Iron Dome" batteries defended the country. This is just one of the many operations and wars Israel has fought in order to protect its existence.

Colonel Richard Kemp, CBE, is a British military expert. He was Commander of British Forces in Afghanistan. The following is an extract of an interview with the BBC:

I don't think there has ever been a time in the history of warfare when any army has made more efforts to reduce civilian casualties and deaths of innocent people than the IDF is doing today in Gaza.
Hamas, the enemy they have been fighting, has been trained extensively by Iran and by Hezbollah, to fight among the people, to use the civilian population in Gaza as a human shield.

Questions:
1. What ethical and operational dilemmas are faced by the IDF in the ongoing war on terror?
2. What were the goals of the IDF in the 2009 Operation Cast Lead and Operation Protective Edge in 2014 in Gaza? Were they achieved?

The State of Israel: War and Peace
(1948—present)

Part Two: Peace— "A Light Unto the Nations"

MISCONCEPTION: Israel is the outlaw nation of the earth with the worst compliance with the rule of law.

REALITY: The State of Israel is a beacon of thriving democracy in a region mired in the darkness of totalitarian despotism. Despite having to constantly struggle for its very existence "Israel is among the most committed [nations] to the rule of law" (Dershowitz). Israel has made tremendous advances in many fields such as immigrant absorption, science, technology, medicine and education.

The State of Israel, Part Two

Objectives:

- Discuss what it means for the Jewish people to have a country of "our own."
- Realise what the ingredients are that make Israel special to us.
- Share with others the image of a real Israel, not the one shown in the media, by highlighting Israel's incredible achievements in the fields of science, technology and medicine.
- Home: Showcase Israel's unprecedented immigration and absorption successes.
- Focus on Israel as a melting pot for Jews from all over the globe.
- Analyse the state symbols of the one country in the world with a Jewish majority.
- Look at some of the problems and challenges facing Israel in the 21st century.
- Review the life of Ilan Ramon as a representation of how much the State of Israel has developed and progressed.

A: Introduction and Motivation

1. Write on the board the word ISRAEL. Ask students to think for a moment: What images come to their minds when they think of Israel. Or: Ask students who haven't been to Israel what images they imagine they will encounter upon arriving to Israel for the first time? Write your students' responses on the board.
2. See how many responses are positive and how many are negative.
3. Discuss the results with the students.
4. If one's perception of Israel is solely media based then it will invariably be negative. In order to understand the reality of 'our Israel' ideally one should visit or live in Israel. It is vital to explore Israel's achievements in order to comprehend the gap between perception and reality. This culminating unit of the course explores the wonder of Israel.

TUVIA

B: Our Israel: Putting the 'is' back

1. The aim of this course of study has been to restore our pride in Israel and Zionism with a foundation of knowledge. For someone growing up in the seventies, it was easy to be proud of Israel. It was the aftermath of the Six Day War (Unit eight) and the Entebbe Raid (Unit Two). Living in the twenty-first century we need to ask ourselves not only what were the aims of Zionism and have they been achieved, but also, where is Zionism going? Do we still have what it takes? Do we still have the pride? Is Israel a "nation like other nations," a "light unto the nations" (Isaiah, 42:6) or maybe a bit of both?

2. The document *par excellence* that states the Zionistic aims of Israel's founders is Israel's Declaration of Independence (Worksheet #1). Have the students analyse the document and answer the questions that follow it.

3. Discuss Worksheet #2 ("Nurture, Not Nature.") After the students have answered the questions and discussed them, add the following: "After having completed this course of study it is not enough to take an exam and forget about it. We must act and spread the word. We must share our feelings with friends and family. We must help to put the 'is' back in Zionism."

4. Home: Part of the *raison d'être* of the Jewish State is that:

"THE STATE OF ISRAEL will be open for Jewish immigration and for the Ingathering of the Exiles"

(Declaration of Independence)

Before reading through Worksheets #3 & 4 (Operation Moses and Operation Solomon and Yityish (Titi) Aynaw) with the students, recap some relevant statistics on *Aliyah* (immigration) and *klitah* (absorption) such as:

- Between 1948 and 1951 – whilst fighting a war for its survival (Unit Eight) – Israel more than doubled its population. Over 680,000 Jews arrived in these years fleeing from persecution in Arab lands and fleeing the blood-stained soil of Europe. Entire ancient communities were airlifted to Israel (Yemen 1949, "Operation Magic Carpet," – 48,000 Jews; and Iraq 1950, "Operation Ezra and Nechemia" – 125,000 Jews.)
- By the end of the first decade since independence there were no more *ma'abarot* (temporary refugee camps).
- Nearly 1 million Russian Jews moved to Israel in the 1990s.
- In 1991, Israel rescued more than 14,400 Jews from Ethiopia in an emergency airlift that lasted 24 hours.

Suggestion: Show a clip from the film "The Search for Peace 1948–1967" (Moriah Films), dealing with the mass immigration (*Aliyot*) between 1948 and 1951, or a film of "Operation Solomon."

5. Achievements: Distribute worksheets #5 and #7. Ask the students, once they have read them, to do research on the Internet (sites in the appendix), to add facts of their own and share them with the class. Ask them which achievements amazed them the most and made them proud of the Jewish State?

6. Symbols: Assign different groups to research the following symbols of the State and find the Jewish symbolic meaning. Share the results.
   • The Flag
   • The Emblem
   • Currency
   • The Anthem

7. Problems: Examine some of the issues the Jewish State has to grapple with in the 21st century, specifically the problems and challenges of the Israeli Arabs (Worksheet #6) and absorbtion of Ethiopian immigrants (Worksheets 3 and 4). It is important not to look at Israel through rose-coloured glasses, but to realise that there are major challenges that cannot be ignored. Answer the questions on the worksheet and discuss possible solutions.

8. Culture: Read Worksheet #9 (Idan Raichel, Israel's Good Will Ambassador) and listen to some of Raichel's music in Hebrew and answer the questions on the worksheet. Play contemporary Israeli music in the classroom and analyse the lyrics in order to expose the students to popular culture in Israel.

9. Ilan Ramon: If one person sums up the achievements of Israel and illustrates just how far Israel has come, that person could be Ilan Ramon (1954–2003) – Worksheet #8.

• Ilan was born in the first decade of the State's existence. His mother and grandmother were both survivors of Auschwitz and arrived in Israel to rebuild their shattered lives.

• His father fought in the War of Independence (Unit Eight) to allow his family to live in peace and security in the new Jewish State.

• Ilan, during his service in the Israeli Air Force, when asked if he would take part in a mission to bomb Iraq's nuclear reactor in 1981 responded: "If I can help prevent a second Holocaust, I'm prepared to sacrifice my life for this." Ilan successfully completed this mission. He also became the first Israeli in space. His mission was deeply symbolic.

• The son of a Holocaust survivor, a colonel in the Israeli Air Force, reaching for the stars, he symbolised just how far Israel has come in a short span of time. A fitting eulogy for such a hero can be found in the words of Chana Szenesh:

"There are stars whose radiance
*   is visible on earth*
though they have long been extinct.
There are people whose brilliance
*   continues to light the world*
though they are no longer among the
*   living.*
These lights are particularly bright
*   when the night is dark.*
They light the way for mankind."

Conclusion

"The message that the Jewish state is about the triumph of possibility over devastation, of life over death, permeates Israel's national culture." *

– Daniel Gordis

Concluding assignment suggestion: Throughout this guide we have focused on heroic men and women who helped shape the Zionist dream. Have students choose the three individuals who have moved and impressed them the most. Write an essay on their achievements stating which of their attributes they will endeavour to include in their own lives as proud and strong Jews and Zionists. One of the concluding "Heroes of Zion" in this guide is Ilan Ramon, Israel's first astronaut.

TUVIA

Ilan Ramon's mission demonstrated that Israel can go anywhere. He reminded us that we have revived our language, made the desert bloom, rebuilt our homeland, ingathered our exiles, have the ability to defend our homeland and protect Jews worldwide and we continue to reach for the stars. In his address to Israeli Prime Minister Ariel Sharon from the Shuttle Columbia in space, he said, "I think we have a great people in Israel, and we have to maintain our Jewish heritage. I think it's very important to preserve our historical and religious traditions." He added that his mission symbolised, "more than anything the ability of the Jewish people to survive anything, including horrible periods, and go from the darkest days to days of hope and faith in the future."

"A new light will shine upon Zion"

(Liturgy)

"אור חדש על ציון תאיר"

(הסידור)

---

* Gordis, Daniel, *Saving Israel, How the Jewish People Can Win a War that May Never End*, (Wiley: USA, 2010)

Name: _____ Date: _____

The Declaration of the Establishment of the State of Israel, May 14, 1948

TUVIA

On May 14, 1948, on the day in which the British Mandate over Palestine expired, the Jewish People's Council gathered at the Tel Aviv Museum, and approved the following proclamation, declaring the establishment of the State of Israel. The new state was recognised that night by the United States and three days later by the U.S.S.R.

Text:

ERETZ-ISRAEL [the Land of Israel, Palestine] was the birthplace of the Jewish people. Here their spiritual, religious and political identity was shaped. Here they first attained to statehood, created cultural values of national and universal significance and gave to the world the eternal Book of Books.

After being forcibly exiled from their land, the people kept faith with it throughout their Dispersion and never ceased to pray and hope for their return to it and for the restoration in it of their political freedom.

Impelled by this historic and traditional attachment, Jews strove in every successive generation to re-establish themselves in their ancient homeland. In recent decades they returned in their masses. Pioneers, *ma'apilim* [– immigrants coming to *Eretz-Israel* in defiance of restrictive British legislation] and defenders, they made deserts bloom, revived the Hebrew language, built villages and towns, and created a thriving community controlling its own economy and culture, loving peace but knowing how to defend itself, bringing the blessings of progress to all the country's inhabitants, and aspiring towards independent nationhood.

In the year 5657 (1897), at the summons of the spiritual father of the Jewish State, Theodor Herzl, the First Zionist Congress convened and proclaimed the right of the Jewish people to national rebirth in its own country.

This right was recognised in the Balfour Declaration of the 2nd November, 1917, and re-affirmed in the Mandate of the League of Nations which, in particular, gave international sanction to the historic connection between the Jewish people and *Eretz-Israel* and to the right of the Jewish people to rebuild its National Home.

The catastrophe which recently befell the Jewish people – the massacre of millions of Jews in Europe – was another clear demonstration of the urgency of solving the problem of its

continued on next page

homelessness by re-establishing in *Eretz-Israel* the Jewish State, which would open the gates of the homeland wide to every Jew and confer upon the Jewish people the status of a fully privileged member of the comity of nations.

Survivors of the Nazi Holocaust in Europe, as well as Jews from other parts of the world, continued to migrate to *Eretz-Israel*, undaunted by difficulties, restrictions and dangers, and never ceased to assert their right to a life of dignity, freedom and honest toil in their national homeland.

In the Second World War, the Jewish community of this country contributed its full share to the struggle of the freedom and peace-loving nations against the forces of Nazi wickedness and, by the blood of its soldiers and its war effort, gained the right to be reckoned among the peoples who founded the United Nations.

On the 29th November, 1947, the United Nations General Assembly passed a resolution calling for the establishment of a Jewish State in *Eretz-Israel*; the General Assembly required the inhabitants of *Eretz-Israel* to take such steps as were necessary on their part for the implementation of that resolution. This recognition by the United Nations of the right of the Jewish people to establish their State is irrevocable.

This right is the natural right of the Jewish people to be masters of their own fate, like all other nations, in their own sovereign State.

ACCORDINGLY WE, MEMBERS OF THE PEOPLE'S COUNCIL, REPRESENTATIVES OF THE JEWISH COMMUNITY OF *ERETZ-ISRAEL* AND OF THE ZIONIST MOVEMENT, ARE HERE ASSEMBLED ON THE DAY OF THE TERMINATION OF THE BRITISH MANDATE OVER *ERETZ-ISRAEL* AND, BY VIRTUE OF OUR NATURAL AND HISTORIC RIGHT AND ON THE STRENGTH OF THE RESOLU-TION OF THE UNITED NATIONS GENERAL ASSEMBLY, HEREBY DECLARE THE ESTABLISHMENT OF A JEWISH STATE IN *ERETZ-ISRAEL*, TO BE KNOWN AS THE STATE OF ISRAEL.

WE DECLARE that, with effect from the moment of the termination of the Mandate being tonight, the eve of Sabbath, the 6th Iyar, 5708 (15th May, 1948), until the establishment of the elected, regular authorities of the State in accordance with the Constitution which shall be adopted by the Elected Constituent Assembly not later than the 1st October 1948, the Peo-ple's Council shall act as a Provisional Council of State, and its executive organ, the People's Administration, shall be the Provisional Government of the Jewish State, to be called "Israel".

THE STATE OF ISRAEL will be open for Jewish immigration and for the Ingathering of the Exiles; it will foster the development of the country for the benefit of all its inhabitants; it will be based on freedom, justice and peace as envisaged by the prophets of Israel; it will ensure complete equality of social and political rights to all its inhabitants irrespective of religion, race or sex;

It will guarantee freedom of religion, conscience, language, education and culture; it will safeguard the Holy Places of all religions; and it will be faithful to the principles of the Char-ter of the United Nations.

Declaration *page 2 of 3*

WORKSHEET #1

THE STATE OF ISRAEL is prepared to cooperate with the agencies and representatives of the United Nations in implementing the resolution of the General Assembly of the 29th November, 1947, and will take steps to bring about the economic union of the whole of *Eretz-Israel*. 1947, and will take steps to bring about the economic union of the whole of *Eretz-Israel*.

WE APPEAL to the United Nations to assist the Jewish people in the building-up of its State and to receive the State of Israel into the comity of nations.

WE APPEAL – in the very midst of the onslaught launched against us now for months – to the Arab inhabitants of the State of Israel to preserve peace and participate in the upbuilding of the State on the basis of full and equal citizenship and due representation in all its provisional and permanent institutions.

WE EXTEND our hand to all neighboring states and their peoples in an offer of peace and good neighborliness, and appeal to them to establish bonds of cooperation and mutual help with the sovereign Jewish people settled in its own land. The State of Israel is prepared to do its share in a common effort for the advancement of the entire Middle East.

WE APPEAL to the Jewish people throughout the Diaspora to rally round the Jews of *Eretz-Israel* in the tasks of immigration and upbuilding and to stand by them in the great struggle for the realisation of the age-old dream – the redemption of Israel.

PLACING OUR TRUST IN THE ROCK OF ISRAEL, WE AFFIX OUR SIGNATURES TO THIS PROCLAMATION AT THIS SESSION OF THE PROVISIONAL COUNCIL OF STATE, ON THE SOIL OF THE HOMELAND, IN THE CITY OF TEL AVIV, ON THIS SABBATH EVE, THE 5TH DAY OF *IYAR*, 5708 (14TH MAY, 1948).

*Published in the Official Gazette, No. 1 of the 5th *Iyar*, 5708 (14th May, 1948).

Questions:
1. How many thematic sections can you divide the Declaration of Independence into?
2. What sections relate to which units we have studied in our course?
3. Would you have written anything differently?
4. How do you feel about the penultimate paragraph ("We appeal to the Jewish people...")? Is this the reality or do we only rally around Israel in times of crisis? If so, why is this? How can we rectify this situation?
5. In what ways are Israel's founding ideals still practiced?

Declaration *page 3 of 3*

Name: _____   Date: _____

Nurture, Not Nature

Lord Jonathan Sacks, Chief Rabbi Emeritus
of Great Britain and the Commonwealth

The most chilling fact to have emerged in the debate about Diaspora Jewish continuity came from a Brandeis University survey. It showed that the single issue that most energised major donors was the fear that their grandchildren would not be Jewish. It also found that they were unwilling to commit funds to continuity for fear that nothing constructive would be done about the issue.

Nothing could be more disastrous to the future of Jewry than self-fulfilling despair. Nor is any attitude less warranted.

In the age of integration, within one or two generations Jews moved from immigrant poverty to unparalleled success in business, the arts, the professions and academic life. In the era of survival, the State of Israel has become a reality a mere 50 years after Theodor Herzl's dream. Compared to these, the challenge of Jewish continuity is simple. For nearly 4,000 years it was, after all, our specialty.

There is nothing inevitable about the crisis of Jewish identity in the Diaspora. It is the result of a century of bad, if understandable, decisions – one above all: we neglected Jewish education. The result is that we know little about Judaism, and our children know less.

They know about the Holocaust – about how Jews died, not how they live. They know about Israel, but that is somewhere else, not here.

Today's young Diaspora Jews are the most secularly educated and Jewishly illiterate of all time. In the United States, four in ten will receive no Jewish education of any kind. Their knowledge of what previous generations of Jews lived and died for is negligible.

Questions:
1. What is the source of the problem that Rabbi Sacks addresses?
2. What, in your opinion, is the solution?
3. How can this solution be implemented in order to, as Rabbi Sacks states: "Relearn what our ancestors knew – that being Jewish is not a fate but a privilege?"

Name: _____   Date: _____

Operation Moses: From Addis Ababa to Israel

Meskie Shibry Sivan

Ever since I can remember, I wanted to immigrate to Israel. However, we had not always known that the State of Israel even existed. Just the opposite – we used to think that we were the only Jews in the world, and observed our tradition very closely. Our grandparents told us tales about the Land of Israel whenever they could, making us curious about that land and yearn for it. Driven by Zionism, my parents made preparations for their immigration long before Operation Moses happened. As children in Addis Ababa, we listened eagerly to stories about the Mossad, our man in Damascus (Eli Cohen), the Six-Day War, the Entebbe operation – and we were proud.

Different, but so much alike, city and country people, we clung to each other and came to beautiful and difficult Israel.

Our ancient community had arrived home and started its last, but no less difficult journey – absorption. We are only at the beginning of this journey, but we are very excited to celebrate the 50th anniversary of our new-old homeland's independence.

OPERATION SOLOMON: ETHIOPIAN JEWS ARRIVE

The airlift in which Ethiopian Jews were brought to Israel started on a Friday evening. Operation Solomon lasted over 24 hours, during which 36 planes landed in Addis Ababa airport one by one and brought more than 14,400 Jews to Israel. The operation, commanded by Ammon Lipkin-Shahak, was the culmination of Operation Moses, which had started in 1984, when some 8,000 Jews were brought to Israel. The operation was halted at that point because of a press leak, and many families had to wait long years for their reunion.

The civil war in Ethiopia worsened in 1990, as did the situation of the Jews who were left behind. They fled from the battle zones to transit camps in Addis Ababa, where they lived in difficult conditions. The Jewish Agency supported them there and helped them organise and prepare for the immigration to Israel.

In May 1991, when rebels started closing in on Addis Ababa, the Israeli government decided to launch the airlift rescue operation. The U.S. Administration exerted a great deal of pressure on the Ethiopian authorities to permit the Jews to emigrate, and diplomatic contacts were made with the rebel leaders. Eventually, all the parties gave their long-awaited permission

continued on next page

WORKSHEET #3

and the operation got under way. Special units were sent to organise the transfer of the Jews to the airport where, in their best clothes and in an orderly way, they boarded the planes in groups. Several hours later, they arrived in Israel, the land of their dreams. In that operation, El Al Airlines broke a record when over 1,000 people were packed into one jumbo jet.

TUVIA

Questions:

1. How does what Israel accomplished in both Operation Moses and Operation Solomon make you feel about the importance of having a Jewish state?
2. After their Immigration (*aliyah*), how are the Jews from Ethiopia faring in their absorption (*klitah*) into Israel?

Operation Moses: From Addis Ababa to Israel *page 2 of 2*

WORKSHEET #4

Name:_____ Date:_____

A Model Role Model-Yityish (Titi) Aynaw

TUVIA

Yityish (Titi) Aynaw (1992–) was crowned Miss Israel in 2013. She was the first Israeli of Ethiopian origin to achieve this honour. Titi overcame tremendous adversity to become a representative of her adopted country.

Whilst many of Israel's Ethiopian Jewish community can trace their roots in the country to the two dramatic airlifts of 1984 and 1991 (Operations Moses and Solomon), Titi's journey from Ethiopia was quite different. Orphaned at the age of twelve, she came alone to Israel to live with her maternal grandparents. She came without the emotional, social, cultural, and linguistic skills necessary for an easy absorption. Instead of wallowing in self-pity for the harsh lot given to her by life she rose above it, and through sheer grit and determination arrived at the point where she is today. As Titi so expressively stated during an interview with the BBC:

I was raised by my grandmother. Nothing was handed to me on a plate. I had to work very hard and long to achieve things in my life. I felt a responsibility to prove myself in everything I did and to improve myself as well.

It is important to acknowledge that with all of Israel's incredible successes in many fields since its creation, there are issues that Israel is grappling with as it continues to stride in the 21st century. The problems that the Jewish State faces include topics as far-ranging as: security, religion, society, environment, how to harmoniously co-exist with a minority population and immigrant absorption. The last issue, immigrant absorption, has been especially felt by Ethiopian immigrants. After the dramatic rescue from certain death by Israel, which was a fine example of Zionism in action, many Ethiopian Jews still feel marginalised in society. Ms. Aynaw has many role models in her life including Martin Luther King Junior. She stated in a recent interview that:

Martin Luther King fought for justice and equality, and that's one of the reasons I'm here. I want to show that my community has many beautiful qualities that aren't always represented in the media. Israel is a multicultural state. We're diverse and we come from different countries, so we need to show that outwardly.

President Obama, who specifically asked to meet her when he was in Israel, is another one of Titi's role models. Imagine if you told a twelve-year-old orphan in a new country that she would overcome many of her absorption difficulties, serve as an officer in the IDF and be invited to meet with the President of the USA at a State gala, all within less than a decade after her arrival? Only in Israel!

Questions:
1. Despite notable exceptions, such as Titi, why do many Ethiopian Jews still feel marginalised in Israeli society? What can be done about this?
2. What are the important lessons we learn from Titi's life story?

WORKSHEET #5

Name: _____ Date: _____

Israel, the 100th smallest country, with less than ⅟₁₀₀₀th of the world's population, can make claim to the following: *

- Israel has the highest ratio of university degrees per capita in the world.
- Israel is ranked #2 in the world for venture capital funds right behind the U.S. Outside the United States and Canada, Israel has the largest number of NASDAQ listed companies.
- Israel has the highest average living standards in the Middle East. The per capita income in 2000 was over $17,500, exceeding that of the U.K.
- Israel's $100 billion economy is larger than all of its immediate neighbors combined.
- On a per capita basis, Israel has the largest number of biotech start-ups.
- 24 percent of Israel's workforce holds university degrees – ranking third in the industrialized world, after the United States and Holland – and 12% hold advanced degrees.
- Israel is the only country in the world that entered the 21st century with a net gain in its number of trees.
- Israel has more museums per capita than any other country.
- In 1984 and 1991, Israel airlifted over 22,000 Ethiopian Jews at risk in Ethiopia to safety in Israel.
- When Golda Meir was elected Prime Minister of Israel in 1969, she became the world's second elected female leader in modern times.
- When the U.S. Embassy in Nairobi, Kenya was bombed in 1998, Israeli rescue teams were on the scene within a day – and saved victims from the rubble.
- Following the devastating 2010 earthquake in Haiti Israel built advanced field hospitals and saved many lives.
- Israel has the third highest rate of entrepreneurship – and the highest rate among women and among people over 55 – in the world.
- Relative to its population, Israel is the largest immigrant-absorbing nation on earth. Immigrants come in search of democracy, religious freedom, and economic opportunity.
- Israel was the first nation in the world to adopt the Kimberly process, an international standard that certifies diamonds as "conflict free."
- According to industry officials, Israel designed the airline industry's most impenetrable flight security. U.S. officials now look to Israel for advice on how to handle airborne security threats.

Questions:
1. Why do you think that these achievements are not widely known or reported by the media?
2. Add your own surprising Israel facts to the list.

_____

* sources: www.standwithus.com and www.Israel21c.org

continued on next page

WORKSHEET #6

Name:_____ Date:_____

Challenges Facing Israel in the 21st Century: Israeli Arabs

It is important to acknowledge that with all of Israel's incredible successes in many fields since its creation, there are issues that Israel is grappling with as it continues to stride into the 21st century.

The problems that the Jewish State faces include topics as far-ranging as: security, religion, society, environment, water, education and how to harmoniously co-exist with a minority population.

The last issue, Israel's minority population, Israeli Arabs, raises a number of interesting points: *

- Approximately 20% of the population consist of Israeli Arabs.
- Of the 20%, about 8% are Druze, about 5% are Bedouin, and about 10% are Christian.
- The Arab minority in Israel are descendents of the pre-Independence community of British Mandatory Palestine who remained within the borders of the State of Israel after its creation.
- Israeli Arabs have full democratic rights.
- Despite their full democratic rights, the resources given to Israeli Arabs are less than those given to the Jews.
- The majority do not serve in the IDF. (The Druze, with mandatory conscription, and Bedouin who can, and do, volunteer are the exception.)
- The non-service in the army results in most Israeli Arabs being denied substantial social benefits.
- At times of recession and unemployment in the Israeli economy, the Israeli Arab sector is consistently amongst the hardest hit.
- Despite the loyalty demonstrated by the vast majority of Israeli Arabs, the number of Israeli Arabs involved in anti-Israel activities, either directly or indirectly, has increased in recent years.
- In recent years, some of the more radical rhetoric of Arab Knesset members has received intense criticism and brought a number of legal probes.
- The self-identity of Israeli Arabs is increasingly showing more overt identification with the Palestinians.

Questions:
1. How do you think Jews should relate to minorities when they become a sovereign majority?
2. What two identities are the Israeli Arab population caught between?
3. What problems and challenges do you think the Israeli Arab minority encounter within the Jewish Zionist State?

_____

* Source: Steve Israel, Connecting to *Community, Jewish Peoplehood, Belonging and Commitment*, (JAFI: Jerusalem, 2003)

continued on next page

WORKSHEET #7

Name:_____ Date:_____

Israeli Achievements in the Fields of Medicine and Technology *

- Israeli scientists developed the first fully computerised, non-radiation, diagnostic instrumentation for breast cancer.

- An Israeli company developed a computerised system for ensuring proper administration of medications, thus removing human error from medical treatment. (Every year in U.S. hospitals, 7,000 patients die from treatment mistakes.)

- Israel's Givun imaging developed the first ingestible video camera, so small it fits inside a pill. Used to view the small intestine from the inside, the camera helps doctors diagnose cancer and digestive disorders.

- Researchers in Israel developed a new device that directly helps the heart pump blood, an innovation with the potential to save lives among those with congestive heart failure. The new device is synchronised with the heart's mechanical operations through a sophisticated system of sensors.

- In response to serious water shortages, Israeli engineers and agriculturalists developed a revolutionary drip irrigation system to minimise the amount of water used to grow crops.

- Israel has the highest percentage in the world of home computers per capita.

- Israel leads the world in the number of scientists and technicians in the workforce, with 145 per 10,000, as opposed to 85 in the U.S., over 70 in Japan, and fewer than 60 in Germany. With over 25% of its work force employed in technical professions. Israel places first in this category as well.

- The cellular phone was developed in Israel by Motorola, which has its largest development center in Israel.

- Most of the Windows NT operating system was developed by Microsoft-Israel.

- The Pentium MMX Chip technology was designed in Israel at Intel. Voice mail technology was developed in Israel.

- Both Microsoft and Cisco built their only R&D facilities outside the U.S. in Israel.

- The technology for AOL Instant Messenger was developed in 1996 by four young Israelis.

- A new acne treatment developed in Israel, the ClearLight device, produces a high-intensity, ultraviolet-light-free, narrow-band blue light that causes acne bacteria to self-destruct – all without damaging surroundings skin or tissue.

- An Israeli company was the first to develop and install a large-scale solar-powered and fully functional electricity generating plant, in southern California's Mojave Desert.

Question:
Which of the above achievements surprised you the most?

_____

* sources: www.standwithus.com and www.israel21c.org

Name: _____   Date: _____

Ilan Ramon (1954–2003) – The First Israeli Astronaut

TUVIA

ILAN RAMON, Colonel in the Israeli Air Force, was born on June 20th, 1954 in Tel Aviv. On January 16th, 2003 he entered the Columbia space shuttle for a 16-day mission. On re-entry, on February 1st, 2003, just 16 minutes before its scheduled landing at Kennedy Space Center in Florida, Columbia broke up in the skies over Texas. All seven crew members died, including Israeli astronaut Ilan Ramon. Ilan Ramon left a wife, Rona, and four children.

Ilan Ramon grew up in Beer Sheva and was considered an outstanding student. During the Yom Kippur War (1973) Ramon was in pilot training. In 1974, Ramon graduated as a fighter pilot from the Israel Air Force Flight School. In 1981 he helped plan and took part in the Israeli attack on the Iraqi nuclear reactor. He fought in the "Operation Peace for Galilee" (1982) War.

In 1997, he was selected as a Payload Specialist and was designated to train for a Columbia Space Shuttle Mission with a payload that included a multispectral camera for recording desert aerosol effects on the climate of the Middle East.

Ramon's sixteen days in space started on January 16th, 2003. On board were six Americans, Rick D. Husband, Michael P. Anderson, David Brown, Kalpana Chawla, Laurel Blair Salton Clark, William C. McCool and Ilan Ramon, the first Israeli in space.

Ramon took several special items with him into space, including: an Israeli flag, a copy of the Israeli Declaration of Independence, a copy of picture from Yad Vashem of the earth seen from the moon as imagined and drawn by 14-year-old Peter Ginz, who was murdered in Auschwitz, a *kiddush* cup for *Shabbat*, a *Sefer Torah* smuggled out of the Bergen Belsen concentration camp, a *mezuzah*, the entire *Tanach* on microfilm, the Jewish Traveler's Prayer and a T-Shirt from the Israeli Road Safety Campaign.

Postscript: On September 13th, 2009 Ilan and Rona Ramon's oldest son, Asaf Ramon, who, following his fathers footsteps, was an F16 pilot in the Israeli Air Force, was killed in a training accident.

Questions:

1. Ilan said that the articles he brought with him to space would "emphasise the unity of the people of Israel and the Jewish communities abroad." What do you think of the articles he took with him?
2. What would you have taken on a mission to space representing the Jewish people and the Jewish State?

WORKSHEET #9

Name: _____ Date: _____

Idan Raichel (1977–): Israel's Good-Will Ambassador

TUVIA

Anyone who has attended an Idan Raichel Project concert will be familiar with witnessing an incredibly participatory audience who leave the performance feeling energised and with a glow of enthusiasm for Israeli culture. The groups blend of African, Latin American, Caribbean and Middle Eastern sounds, coupled with a spectacular live show, has enchanted audiences worldwide. Indeed the Idan Raichel Project has boldly gone to geographical locations no other Israeli performers have gone before. This trail-blazing enterprise has helped raise global awareness to a sound that reflects our Zionist state's multi-ethnic and tolerant makeup that exists beyond the headlines.

Raichel says that he considers it a great honour to bring a taste of Israel to other countries. When asked by the *New York Times* why he has so many Biblical lyrics in his songs he replied:

> *I use the Bible because all the most important and beautiful things have already been said, so that the best that I can probably do is repeat them…there is simply no greater love song than what you find in the Book of Psalms.*

Raichel's infectious enthusiasm for the multi-cultural and multi-ethnic melting pot represented by the State of Israel is reflected in his music. Usually the first thing that enters people's minds upon hearing the word "Israel" is, "conflict" (or falafel). Israel needs to move its image beyond the conflict. The Project, and the positive energy and good will that it globally disseminates, make it one of Israel's most effective ambassadors. The *Hasbara* value is priceless.

Yet with all the talk about globalism and world music Idan Raichel is very clear that home is where the heart is, and his heart is very much in Israel. Having served in the IDF himself, which he refers to as a "basic Ingredient" to "Israeliness," he made a very moving observation about the two-minute silence during Memorial Day (*Yom Hazikaron*):

> *I think that those two minutes truly reflect the Israeli way of life, the Israeli pride, our longing and sadness, our concern for and about the future, our patriotism and our mutual destiny. Those two minutes truly show what all Israelis have in common, if it's our lives in the present, or the respect we have for our past. To me, those two minutes sharpen our minds and are the epitome of Israeli society.*

Questions:
1. After having listened to Raichel's music, what do you think makes it so internationally appealing?
2. Why does Raichel refer to the IDF as the basic ingredient to "Israeliness?" Do you agree with his statement?

Name:_____ Date:_____

Israel Education, Jewish Identity and the Israel Experience Trip

One of the proven paths focusing on an enhanced understanding of Israel to strengthen Jewish identity is the Israel experience trip. Gil Troy notes that there is; "a positive association between a visit to Israel and measures of Jewish identification, community affiliation and religious practice." David Mittelberg, concurring with Troy and numerous other researchers, claims that, "An Israel visit continues to reflect or to serve as an extra powerful element in the Jewish identity of the individual."

His point is that the strength and nature of one's connection with Israel is often used as an indicator of Jewish identity among Diaspora Jews. An Israel experience complements both Jewish identity formation and Israel education providing that the Israel experience focuses on Israel as a modern dynamic society full of rich diversity and issues it is facing and grappling with, then there is great potential for the participant's personal connections to Judaism and the Jewish State.

Steven Cohen's research considers differences in identification and identity between Israeli and American Jews, as well as between American Jews who have visited Israel and those who have not. His results indicate that the relationship between the Israel education and Jewish identity is so significant that placing an Israel trip on the Jewish/Israel education agenda, according to Cohen, "may be the most policy relevant action organized Jews can undertake to stem the erosion in Israel attachment (and resulting Jewish identity) among younger adult Jews"

Cohen's survey specifically concluded that the impact of an Israel trip is essential for fortifying Jewish identity and commitment and preventing alienation from Israel and the Jewish faith. This is clearly more significant for younger people. The research would seem to lend credence to the commonly held belief that an "Israel experience" will reverse the tendency among younger Diaspora Jews to be more distant from Israel, and the Jewish faith, and will indeed help reinforce their engagement with both Judaism and the Jewish State.

Question:
Why do think it is so important to visit Israel, preferably on a peer educational trip, in order to develop a clear understanding regarding the achievements and challenges facing Israel?

Chronology

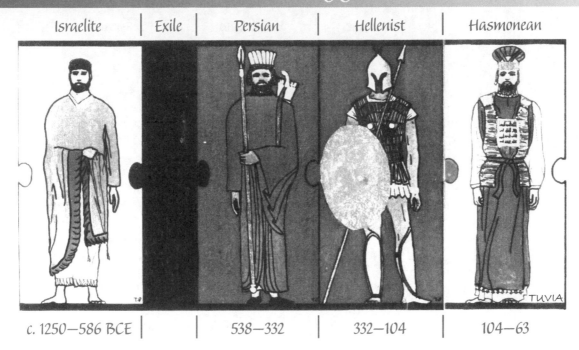

Israelite	Exile	Persian	Hellenist	Hasmonean
c. 1250–586 BCE		538–332	332–104	104–63

C. 2000–1750 BCE	Patriarchs and Matriarchs
C. 1750–1400 BCE	First Exile – Slavery in Egypt
C. 1400–1250 BCE	Exodus and return Home, Moses receives the Torah at Sinai
C. 1250–1050 BCE	Conquest of Canaan; Joshua leads, followed by the Judges
C. 1030–1006 BCE	The reign of Saul, first Israelite King
C. 1006- 965 BCE	David rules, establishes Jerusalem as the capital
C. 965–930 BCE	Solomon rules, builds the First Temple in Jerusalem
C. 925 BCE	Division of the United Kingdom, North (Israel) and South (Judah)
722 BCE	Fall of the northern kingdom to Assyria
586 BCE	Destruction of First Temple by Babylonians
536 BCE	Decree of Cyrus allows Jews to return to Israel, but many stay in Babylonia
520–515 BCE	Jews rebuild Temple under Ezra and Nechemia
C. 332 BCE	Alexander the Great establishes Greek Rule throughout the Near East
C. 200 BCE	Hebrew Bible standardized and divided into Torah, Prophets, and Writings
168–165 BCE	Maccabean Revolt against Antiochus IV (the story of Chanuka)
63 BCE	Pompey invades and Roman rule of Judea begins
37–4 BCE	Herod governs Judea
C. 29 CE	Jesus crucified by Romans in Jerusalem
70	Fall of Jerusalem, Temple destroyed, Yohanan Ben Zakkai escapes to Yavneh
73	Fall of Masada
132–135	Second revolt in Judea against Rome, led by Simon Bar Kochba
135	Hadrian renames Judea, Syria-Palestina (Palestine)
C. 390	Jerusalem Talmud completed
C. 500	Babylonian Talmud completed
570–635	Mohammed founds Islam
638	Arabs conquer Jerusalem

Chronology

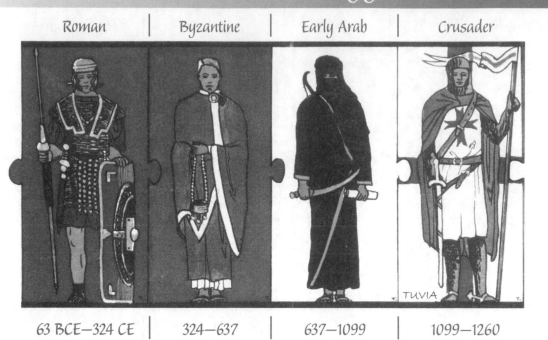

Roman	Byzantine	Early Arab	Crusader
63 BCE—324 CE	324—637	637—1099	1099—1260

1040–1105	Rashi, the great Torah commentator, lives in Troyes, France
1075–1141	Judah HaLevi, the Spanish poet, whose heart is in the East
1096–1099	First Crusade
1135–1204	Maimonides, physician, rationalist, innovator, teacher
1348–1349	Black Death devastates Europe, Jews blamed
1492	Jews expelled from Spain
1517	Ottoman Empire conquers Palestine
1534–1572	Rabbi Isaac Luria, Ha'Ari, the great mystic of Safed
1555	Joseph Caro writes the Shulchan Aruch in Safed
1648 – 1649	Chmelnitski Revolt in the Ukraine – Jews massacred
1666	The false messiah Shabbetai Tzvi converts to Islam
1700–1760	The Baal Shem Tov, charismatic leader of the Hasidim
1720–1797	Vilna Gaon, rationalist leader of the Mitnagdim
1729–1786	Moses Mendelssohn, the Great "Maskil"
1791	5 years after French Revolution, Jews declared full citizens
1806	Napoleon's Sanhedrin
1881	Pogroms in Russia
1882	BILU begins the *chalutzic*, pioneering movement to Israel
1894	Dreyfus Affair, French Jewish army captain framed
1896	Theodor Herzl writes *Der Judenstaat,* the Jewish State
1897	First Zionist Congress held at Basel
1903	Kishinev Pogroms – the subject of Bialik's *City of Slaughter* poem
1914–1918	World War One
1921	British partition of Trans-Jordan and Palestine, British Mandate begins
1925	Founding of Hebrew University
1939–1945	World War II and the Holocaust

Chronology

Mameluke	Ottoman	British	Israel
1260—1527	1517—1917	1917—1948	1948 →

1947	UN partitions Palestine. Arab guerillas reject the compromise and attack
1948	State of Israel proclaimed, seven Arab armies attack
1948—1951	Massive immigration doubles Israel's pre-state population
1956	Suez Campaign, Israel forced to withdraw after capturing the Sinai
1967	Six-Day War, pre-emptive strike, Jerusalem reunited
1973	Yom Kippur War, surprise attack
1975	UN declares Zionism is racism
1976	Entebbe raid, 'Operation Jonathan'
1979	Camp David accords between Egypt and Israel signed
1981	The Israeli Air force destroys Iraq's fledgling nuclear reactor
1982	Lebanon War
1989	Mass immigration of Jews from the Soviet Union begins
1991	Rescue of over 14,000 Ethiopian Jews in 'Operation Solomon'
1993	Oslo Accords
1994	Peace with Jordan
1995	Rabin assassinated
2000	Palestinians riot against Oslo
2000	Israel unilaterally withdraws from southern Lebanon
2003	Ilan Ramon, the first Israeli astronaut, travels to space
2004	Gal Friedman wins Israel's first Olympic Gold Medal
2006	Israel unilaterally withdraws from the Gaza strip
2006	Second Lebanon War
2010	Israel is the country with the largest Jewish population in the world
2014	Operation Protective Edge
2018	Israel celebrates 70 years of independence

Bibliography

Recommended books, films and websites to enhance each unit.

Books:

Abbey, Allen D., *Journey of Hope, The Story of Ilan Ramon – Israel's First Astronaut* (Gefen: New York / Jerusalem, 2003) [Unit: 9]

Bard, Mitchell E., *Myths and Facts, A Guide to the Arab-Israel Conflict,* (AICEI: USA, 2001) [Units: 8, 9]

Begin, Menachem, *The Revolt,* (Steimatsky: Jerusalem, 1991) [Unit: 7]

Ben-Sasson H., Haim, ed. *A History of the Jewish People,* (Harvard: Cambridge, 1985) [Unit: 2]

Collins, Larry and Lapierre, Dominique, *O Jerusalem!,* (Simon and Schuster, NY, 1988) [Units: 7, 8]

Dershowitz, Alan, *The Case for Israel,* (John Wiley and Sons: USA, 2003) [Units: 2, 7, 8, 9]

Gilbert, Martin, *Israel – A History,* (Black Swan: London, 1999) [Units: 4–9]

Gilbert, Martin, *The Arab-Israel Conflict – Its History in Maps,* (W & N: London, 1992) [Unit: 8]

Gordis, Daniel, *Saving Israel, How the Jewish People Can Win a War that May Never End,* (Wiley: USA, 2010) [Units 8,9]

Hazony, Yoram, *The Jewish State: the Struggle for Israel's Soul,* (Basic Books: NY, 2001) [Unit: 9]

Herzberg, Arthur, *The Zionist Idea: An Historical Analysis and Reader,* (JPS: NY, 1997) [Unit: 8]

Katz, Yossi, *A Voice Called, Stories of Jewish Heroism,* (Gefen: Jerusalem/New York, 2010/5770) [Units: 7, 8]

Lacquer, Walter, *A History of Zionism,* (Tauris Parke: NY, 2003 [Units: 1, 4, 5]

Lossin, Yigal, *Pillar of Fire,* (Shikmona: Jerusalem, 1992) [Units: 4–7]

Mendes-Flohr, Paul R. and Jehuda Reinharz, eds., *The Jew in the Modern World: A Documentary History,* (Oxford: New York, 1980) [Units: 4, 8]

Netanyahu, Benjamin, *A Durable Peace, Israel and its Place Amongst the Nations,* (Warner: New York, 2000) [Unit: 9]

Netanyahu, Jonathan, *The Letters of Jonathan Netanyahu.* (Gefen: NY and Israel, 2002) [Unit: 2]

O'Brien, Conor Cruise, *The Siege,* (Simon and Schuster: New York, 1988) [Units: 4–9]

Oren, Michael, *Six Days of War, June 1967 and the Making of the Modern Middle East,* (Oxford: USA, 2002) [Unit: 8]

Peters, Joan, *From Time Immemorial,* (Harper & Row: New York, 1984) [Unit: 8]

Segev, Tom, *One Palestine Complete – Jews and Arabs under the British Mandate,* (Henry Holt and Company: New York, 2000) [Units: 6, 7]

Senor, Dan, and Saul Singer, *Start Up Nation, The Story of Israel's Economic Miracle,* (Twelve: New York, 2009) [Unit: 9]

Shavit, Ari, *My Promised Land, The Triumph and Tragedy of Israel,* (Spiegel & Grau, 2013) [Units: 4–9]

Szenesh, Chana, *Chana Szenesh Her Life and Diary,* (Jewish Lights: New York, 2009) [Unit: 7]

Singer, Alex, *Alex: Building a Life – the Story of an American Who Fell Defending Israel,* (Gefen: New York & Jerusalem, 1996) [Unit: 8]

Telushkin, Joseph, *Jewish Literacy: The Most Important Things to Know About the Jewish Religion, Its People, and Its History,* (William Morrow and Company, Inc.: New York, 2008)

Troy, Gil, *Why I am a Zionist – Israel, Jewish Identity and the Challenges of Today,* (Bronfman Jewish Education Center: Montreal, 2006) [Units: 1, 2, 9]

Uris, Leon, *Exodus* (Turtleback: New York, 1989) [Unit: 7]

Wiesel, Elie, *Dawn,* (Bantam: New York, 2000) [Unit 7]

Websites

Useful Web Sites on Israel – Media

In these times it is vital to be informed on current events in Israel in a clear, concise and accurate manner. This information will enable us to respond with logic, calm, and above all, truth to criticism that is falsely heaped upon Israel.

- **www.honestreporting.com**
  Protest biased coverage of Israel in the media.
  It offers comprehensive media links for reporting Israel – from both sides.
- **www.jpost.com**
  Find out about current events in Israel through the internet edition of the Jerusalem Post: or the Jerusalem Report – www.jrep.com .
- **www.camera.com**
  Learn about how Israel is reported in the media (and understand how the news we read and see often misrepresents the actual events) by learning about an organisation called the Committee for Accuracy in Middle East Reporting in America.
- **www.debka.com**
  Dig "behind the scenes" for information devoted to representing Israel's point of view.
- **www.memri.org**
  Discover what the Arab world is saying. The Middle East Media and Research Institute, (MEMRI), website. An independent, non-profit organisation providing translations of the Arab media and original analysis and research on developments in the Middle East.
- **www.kolisrael.com**
  Tune in to Radio, News, Sports and Arts from Israel
- **www.mideasttruth.com**
  Spread the truth about the Middle East conflict.
- **www.nationalreview.com/hanson/hanson050702.asp**
  Analyse three fallacies upon which modern hatred of Israel is based. ("Hating Israel," National Review By Victor Davis Hanson.)
- **www.pmw.org.il**
  Understand the Palestinian Authority's views on Jews, Israel, and America in their own words translated from their TV, newspapers, and radio.
- **www.myisraelsource.com**
  Discover all Israel news, not just the terror. This site gathers information from several of the world's leading news sources including: The New York Times, Ha'aretz, The Jerusalem Post, and The Jewish Telegraphic Agency. The "Links" section is extensive and useful.

Websites

Useful Web Sites on Israel – Social Action

Things you can do to make a positive difference:

- **www.ujc.org/wjewry_home.html**
  Find ideas on helping Israel ranging from missions to education.
- **www.birthrightisrael.com**
  Travel free with birthright israel which provides a gift of first time, peer group, educational trips to Israel for Jewish young adults ages 18 to 26
- **www.aipac.org/Action1.cfm**
  Send letters or e-mails to the President, senators and your congressperson asking them to support Israel. You can learn more about doing this through the national American Israel Political Action Committee.
- **www.jafi.org.il/ed/**
  Learn all about Israel with your family. There are all sorts of resources, including maps of Israel, historical information, and ideas for Israel activism and learning at the Jewish Agency for Israel.
- **www.jafi.org.il/daily/vol.asp**
  Volunteer for Israel Now! Volunteer Opportunities: 2–4 week programs for ages 18 to 65. Physicians, MDA (Magen David Adom), Maintenance and Supply Services, Kibbutz Volunteers, Work with Children with Special Needs, Civil Guard Qualifications: ENTHUSIASM AND LOVE OF ISRAEL! To register, please see site information.
- **www.mia.org.il**
  Work for the release of Missing Israeli Soldiers. This comprehensive site from a private organisation, The International Coalition for Missing Israeli Soldiers (ICMIS), is dedicated to the Israeli MIAs from the 1980s until today. Includes updates, chronology, photos, vigil information, a petition and more.
- **info.jpost.com/1999/Supplements/Education/**
  Study in Israel. This site contains details and information of many High School and College long and short-term study programs.
- **www.amiie.org**
  Broaden your horizons. During this 8-week unique academic adventure at Alexander Muss High School in Israel you will see things that stir your emotions and learn things that touch your soul.
- **Join a Zionist Youth Movement** – here is a list of movement websites covering all denominations:
  www.bneiakiva.org Bnei Akiva
  www.habonimdror.org Habonim Dror
  hashomerhatzair.org Hashomer Hatzair
  www.jccmaccabix.org JCC/Maccabi
  www.nfty.org NFTY (North American Federation of Temple Youth)
  www.usy.org USY (United Synagogue Youth)
  www.youngjudaea.org Young Judaea

Websites

Useful Web Sites on Israel – Education Sites and Material

- **www.jajz-ed.org.il/jerusalem/activities.html**
  Learn everything you want to know about Jerusalem including: activities for youth and teens, sermon ideas, timeline, a lengthy bibliography for further research, numerous web links, FAQs about the kotel, maps, places in Jerusalem, and more! This site is in English, Hebrew, Russian and German.

- **www.jecc.org**
  Introduce a mini-response curriculum from the Curriculum Resources Department of the Jewish Education Center of Cleveland (JECC) to your school in order to help teachers better respond to the varied emotions emerging from the current situation in Israel.

- **www.jewishagency.org.il/ed/**
  Learn all about Israel with your family. There are all sorts of resources, including maps of Israel, historical information, and ideas for Israel activism and learning at the Jewish Agency for Israel

- **www.jajz-ed.org.il/100/maps/index.html**
  Use maps to put the Middle East conundrum into perspective.

- **www.aish.com/jewishissues/middleeast/The-Occupied_Territories-A_Primer. asp**
  Understand the power of words: "Occupied" or "disputed" territories? The difference is enormous. Here's everything you need to know.

- **www.jajz-ed.org.il/dept/news/ambassador.html**
  Use "The Ambassador" course to empower you in the facts of the conflict, the tools to understand Palestinian propaganda/media bias and the means to advocate Israel.

- **www.yourpage.org/teachers.html**
  Download great ideas to make Israel lesson plans exciting and meaningful.

- **www.archpark.org.il**
  Visit the Jerusalem Archaeological Park which contains state-of-the-art technology portraying virtual reconstructions of Jerusalem during its long history.

- **www.jajz-ed.org.il/shlichim/jzionistsem/zionisimpage1.html#sem**
  Bring Israelis into your school. The "*Achai VeRe'ai*" programs are staffed by college-age experienced informal educators who have undergone professional training in all methods of informal education including art, music, film, drama and games.

- **www.myisraelsource.com/helplet/activities.html**
  Prepare your Israel classes with ease by utilising numerous lesson plan outlines

- **www.davidproject.org**
  Promote understanding of the Middle East conflict. The David Project does not endorse any political agenda beyond Israel's right to exist securely alongside its Arab neighbors.

- **www.standwithus.com**
  Educate yourself about Israel and the misinformation that often surrounds the Middle East conflict. Stand With Us is an international organization dedicated to bringing peace to the Middle East.

Websites

Useful Web Sites on Israel – General Israel-Related Links

- **www.goisrael.com**
  Israel Ministry of Tourism. This site provides regularly updated information specifically geared towards tourists. This service is perfect for people planning trips to Israel or parents with children on Israel programs. Information is given about how the current political climate will or will not affect a tourist's stay in Israel. The site also gives information about various sites and can be used to book your trip.

- **www.idf.il**
  The official site of the IDF provides updated news about the army and soldiers of Israel as well as IDF services, missing soldiers, and other subjects relevant to the IDF. **IDF Special Forces site www.isayeret.com**.

- **www.israelinsider.com**
  Daily updated news about Israel including links to numerous newspapers and editorial content. A particularly good feature is the flash maps and graphs which provide information about the make-up of the Knesset, Israel's borders, disputed territories, and more.

- **www.knesset.gov.il**
  The Knesset: Israeli Parliament. Information about the government, the political system in Israel and individual Members of Knesset (MKs) as well of texts of various laws and other features. The site also has links to other government sites (president, judiciary, etc...) and the means to contact MKs.

- **www.israel-mfa.gov.il**
  Israeli Government official website: The Ministry of Foreign Affairs – Daily news updates from the Foreign Affairs ministry. This site includes "Facts about Israel" which gives a complete history of the Land and State of Israel, information on technology, population, economy, culture, religion, and more.

- **www.nbn.org.il**
  Nefesh B'Nefesh provides Olim with financial assistance, employment resources, assistance with governmental absorption, and community-based guidance and support, in order to make each individual's Aliyah as successful as possible.

- **www.israelemb.org**
  Israeli Embassy in Washington DC

- **www.israelimages.com**
  Photographs and images of Israel

- **www.jnf.org**
  The Jewish National Fund site contains ideas on how to help Israel's environment, Israel Education, donation opportunities, and many other useful items.

- **www.aliyah.org**
  Dreaming of living in Israel? Need answers? Looking for the best way to explore the possibilities? The Israel *Aliyah* Center can help!

- **www.tourism.gov.il/TourHeb/virtual%20tour/index.html**
  Embark on a Virtual Tour of Israel – great photos, lots to see, 360-degree views.

- **www.israel21c.org**
  Beyond the conflict: This site identifies, researches and reports on how Israelis create, innovate, improve and add value to the world.

Films

Suggested Films to Enhance Each Unit:

- **Unit One** *"Crossing the Line 2, The New Face of Anti-Semitism on Campus."* (Jerusalem U 2015, 30 minutes) presents the radical agenda of some pro-Palestinian activists, the misuse of the student government, and the precariousness of free speech on campus today.

- **Unit Two** *Follow Me, The Yoni Netanyahu Story* (Crystal City 2012, 87 minutes) brings a rare portrait of Israel's elite soldiers and their greatest hero to the big screen.

- **Unit Four** *Pillar of Fire, Part I* (ITV, Keshet Productions, 50 minutes) "The Jew Return / The Arab Awakens (1896–1920)" examines the *Chalutzim*, WWI and Arab nationalism.

- **Unit Five** *Pillar of Fire, Part IV* (ITV, Keshet Productions, 50 minutes) "Who's Afraid of a Jewish State? (1937–1939)" examines the Arab revolt against the British and the Jews.

  "Israel Inside, How a Small Nation Makes a Difference." (Jerusalem U 2011, 55 minutes) examines the core character strengths that have enabled Israelis to overcome challenges and turn a barren desert into a flourishing nation.

- **Unit Six** *Pillar of Fire, Part II* (ITV, Keshet Productions, 50 minutes, "The Dream (1914 1929)" examines the end of WWI and the Third *Aliyah*.

- **Unit Seven** *The Long Way Home* (Moriah Films 1997, 119 minutes) examines the critical post-World War II period between 1945 and 1948 and the struggle of the tens of thousands of displaced Jewish refugees to find dignity and renewal in the aftermath of the Nazi Holocaust.

  Blessed is the Match, The Life and Death of Hannah Senesh (Katahdin Productions, 2008, 50 minutes) re-enacts the story of Hanna Szenesh, the *Haganah* heroine and poetess who parachuted into Nazi occupied Europe during WWII to rescue Jews, losing her own life at the hands of the Nazi collaborators..

  In Our Own Hands (Chuck Olin 1998, 85 minutes) recounts the amazing adventures of the Jewish Brigade. We see the Brigade fighting the Germans in Italy during WWII. At the same time they also helped European Jewish survivors get to British Mandatory Palestine and smuggled trucks, weapons and ammunition from British war depots to Palestine.

  Exodus (MGM 1960, 220 minutes) recreates the turbulent months of 1947 surrounding the creation of the State of Israel. The film is an epic portrayal of the Jewish struggle against the British Mandatory authorities and hostile Arabs.

- **Unit Eight** *Alex Singer: Building a Life* (Alex Singer Project 1998, 15 minutes) is a compelling portrayal of Alex Singer, an American volunteer in the IDF in the 1980s. It presents Alex's life, art, and writings, including documentary footage illustrating Alex's army service and other periods of his life.

  Cast a Giant Shadow (MGM 1966, 138 minutes) focuses on Israel's difficult struggle for statehood. It is the story of Colonel David "Mickey" Marcus, an American military officer who led the nascent Israeli Army in defense of its newly formed borders and relieved the siege of Jerusalem.

  Beneath the Helmet, From High School to the Home Front (Jerusalem U 2015, 80 minutes) is a coming-of-age story which follows the journey of five Israeli high school graduates who are drafted into the army to defend their country. At the age of 18, away from their homes, families and friends these young individuals undergo a demanding, inspiring journey, revealing the core of who they are and who they want to be.

Map and Photo Index

Michael Levin (z"l), A Hero in Heaven (Sally Mitlas Film Productions 2007, 45 minutes) tells of Michael's devotion to his family, his people and Israel in a unique and powerful way, through the music of Naomi Shemer, the songs of Rachel, the poems of Tchernokovsky and the words of Michael's family, friends and fellow soldiers who loved him dearly.

- **Unit Nine** *In Search of Peace, Part One 1948–67* (Moriah Films 2001, 112 minutes) not only examines events in Israel, but their impact on other places as well – the Arab refugee camps, the General Assembly of the United Nations and the world capitals.

Space Shuttle Columbia: Mission of Hope (PBS, 2013, 60 minutes) is a moving and important documentary about Ilan Ramon, Israel's first astronaut. It follows his footsteps, examines the achievements of his life and what he symbolised for the Jewish people.

Maps

Illustrations

About the Author

Tuvia Book

Tuvia Book was born in London and raised in both the UK and South Africa. After making Aliyah at the age of 17, and studying in Yeshiva, he volunteered for the IDF where he served in an elite combat unit. Upon his discharge he completed his BA at Bar-Ilan University, as well as certification in graphic design. He then served as the Information Officer at the Israeli Consulate of Philadelphia, while earning a graduate degree in Jewish Studies. Upon his return to Israel, Mr. Book graduated from a course of study with the Israeli Ministry of Tourism, and is a licensed tour guide.

Tuvia has been working in the field of Jewish Education, both formal and informal, for many years. He has guided and taught Jewish students and educators from around the English-speaking world for some of Israel's premier educational institutions and programs. Tuvia has been guiding groups for Birthright Israel since its inception and, in addition, has lectured throughout North America, Australia, Europe and South Africa.

Tuvia served as a *Shaliach* (emissary) for the Jewish Agency for Israel as the Director of Israel and Zionist Education at the Board of Jewish Education of Greater New York. He was a lecturer/educational guide at the Alexander Muss Institute for Israel Education (AMIIE) in Israel for a decade. Tuvia has lectured at both Bar Ilan University and Hebrew University.

Currently Tuvia is a doctoral candidate in Jewish education. He is married to Shira, a physician, and they have four children; Ayelet, Aaron, Aden and Aviv.

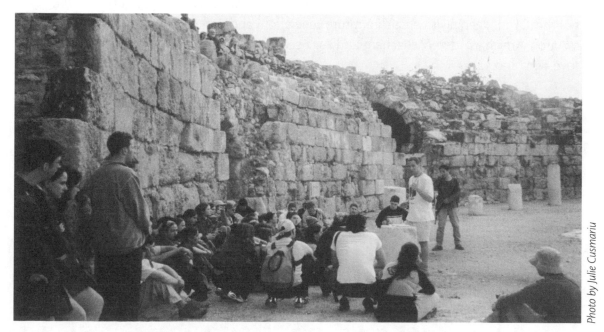

Tuvia guiding a Canadian Birthright Israel *tour at Beit Guvrin*

Photo by Julie Cusmariu

Acknowledgements

From the Jewish Agency for Israel's Department of Jewish and Zionist Education, I would like to thank Dr. Meryl Weisman, for her encouragement and help; Alan Hoffman for his interest; Noga Oz for her support, and I would also like to thank Chaim Weinreb for his enthusiastic backing for this work. Finally, last but not least, from the Research and Development team, Dr Ami Bouganim and Mariana Kronfeld for their help in the second edition.

The Alexander Muss High School in Israel (AMIIE) is where I crystallized many of the ideas in this book. It is a world leader in experiential Jewish Education. I would particularly like to express appreciation to Chaim Fishgrund, Principal emeritus, for granting me permission to use ideas and material I obtained and developed whilst teaching in the school and Yossi Katz for being my mentor.

I would like to thank Sara Ahronheim, Harriet Levin (mother of Michael Levin z"l), Yossi Katz and Chief Rabbi Emeritus, Lord Jonathan Sacks, for permission to use their articles. I would also like to express gratitude to Professor Gil Troy for his enthusiastic support and permission to use quotes and maps from his book *Why I am a Zionist – Israel Jewish Identity and the Challenges of Today* (BJEC 2006). I would also like to thank Dr. Shira R. Alter, Charlton Book, Margaret Book, Robin Deutsch Edwards, Melissa Weiner Wolchansky, and Channa K. Miller for their editing skills. I would like to express my gratitude to Nina Woldin whose artistic eye and Raphaël Freeman whose layout skills helped make this book so aesthetically pleasing.

Finally, this book could not have been written without the love and support of my family. My Father and mother, Rabbi Dr. Leonard and Margaret Book, who raised me to be a proud and strong Jew and Zionist and encouraged the *Aliyah* of their children, and my mother-in-law, Susan Alter, and sister-in-law, Beth H. Alter for their support. Many thanks to my siblings: Charlton, Temima, Avigdor Ziv and Saranne. I am especially indebted to my wife Shira. This book is dedicated to the soldiers of the IDF for keeping Israel safe for future generations and to our darling children, Ayelet Yehudit, Aaron Amichai, Aden Menachem and Aviv Leor. May they grow up in a world full of peace, love, light and joy.

"A new light will shine on Zion and may
we all soon be worthy to enjoy it"

"אור חדש על ציון תאיר וזכה כולנו מהרה לאורו"

TUVIA

"My mission symbolises more than anything the ability of the Jewish people to survive anything, including horrible periods, and go from the darkest days to days of hope and faith in the future."

(Ilan Ramon 1954–2003)